D0224257

PORTFOLIOS
—FOR—
DEVELOPMENT

To Susan with best wishes Warren Redman

PORTFOLIOS

—— FOR ——

DEVELOPMENT

A Guide for Trainers and Managers

W a r r e n   R e d m a n

Kogan Page Ltd, London
Nichols Publishing Company,
New Jersey

First published in 1994
Reprinted 1995

Apart from any fair dealing for the purposes of research or private study, or
criticism or review, as permitted under the Copyright, Designs and Patents
Act, 1988, this publication may only be reproduced, stored or transmitted, in
any form or by any means, with the prior permission in writing of the
publishers, or in the case of reprographic reproduction in accordance with the
terms of licences issued by the Copyright Licensing Agency. Enquiries
concerning reproduction outside those terms should be sent to the publishers at
the undermentioned address:

Kogan Page Limited
120 Pentonville Road
London N1 9JN

©Warren Redman, 1994

British Library Cataloguing in Publication Data

A CIP record for this book is available from the British Library.

ISBN 0 7494 1158 9

Published in the USA by Nichols Publishing
PO Box 6036, East Brunswick, NJ 08816

Library of Congress Cataloging-in-Publication Data

Redman. Warren.
    Portfolios for development : a guide for trainers and managers /
Warren Redman.
        p. cm.
    Includes bibliographical references and index.
    ISBBN 0-89397-394-7 (pb.) : $27.95
    1. career development.   I. Title.
HF5549.5.C35R43   1994
658.3' 124—dc20   93-42470
                                                              CIP

Typeset by Books Unlimited (Nottm), Sutton-in-Ashfield, NG17 1AL

Printed and bound in Great Britain by Biddles Limited, Guildford and King's
Lynn.

Contents

Acknowledgements

There are a number of organizations referred to in this book. I would like to thank them all for letting me work with them and for allowing me to quote some of the experience they have had of portfolio development.

They are:

CCDU, The University of Leeds;
The Grove Management Centre (British Rail);
National Association of Citizen's Advice Bureaux
(Merseyside and West Cheshire);
Nottinghamshire County Council;
Sandwell Metropolitan Borough Council;
Sutcliffe Catering Group Ltd (thanks also for permission to quote from *Learning from Experience*, reproduced on pages 115–16).

Chapter 1

Introduction

To start with

It started, as so many things do, with a phone call. The date was October 1985; the call was from the training and development director of a national voluntary organization with whom I had worked on a number of projects in the past. 'I'm on a working party whose task is to investigate the use of portfolios in training within the youth service', he said. 'We're looking for someone to carry out the work on our behalf. Would you be interested?'

I had no real idea what he was talking about. What I did know was that the voluntary youth service in the UK was always willing to experiment with new approaches. I could learn a lot and maybe be a part of some new development. So I said yes, I'd be interested, but I'd have to know a lot more first.

Over the following three years I found out a great deal. The Portfolio Project was based on the premise that people bring with them to their work, whether paid or voluntary, a great deal of knowledge, skills and understanding that is seldom properly recognized or acknowledged. The implication of this was to turn training on its head for many youth service organizations. Instead of running basic and continuing training courses on the assumption that adults coming in to work with young people had little or no experience, organizations like the Scout Association would invite their volunteer workers to build a portfolio of past experience and negotiate a training programme relevant to their needs.

This made a lot of sense. I and many of my colleagues had been working in a similar way for years, but it had been hard to get the approach accepted in a formal way. By 1989 the ideas and some of the practice had spread to about ten of the major national youth organizations and to a larger number of youth service departments in local government authorities. The effect was startling and satisfying and convinced me that here was something of potentially powerful value to anyone interested in the development of people within organizations.

I started talking portfolios. I spoke to people in other, different kinds of organizations; to managers and trainers in large and small businesses, in public service organizations, to local government officers. Interest slowly grew.

This book has grown out of that interest and the practical work that individuals and organizations have done in developing themselves through building portfolios. Like the concept of portfolio-building, the book is based on practical experience, laced with the thinking behind and the results of that experience. Now, almost overnight, trainers, managers and developers have become aware of portfolio development as an idea, linking it to the requirements imposed by National Vocational Qualifications and the Management Charter Initiative. My aim in writing this book is to describe what a portfolio is, what it can do, and how it can be used to develop individuals, teams and organizations.

There is a training revolution taking place through the setting up of NVQs and the MCI. The results will be profound. Some will be positive, others negative to the point of making the whole thing a disastrous waste of time, energy and money. Portfolio development, properly understood and carried out, can prevent the worst of the potential excesses and help to ensure that the best practice really is the best possible. That means using the portfolio approach as a way towards continual learning. If individuals can learn from their experience, synergy within organizations indicates that we can learn corporately even more effectively. The task is always to ensure that, as far as possible, the experience and what is learnt from it is seen as positive.

What I will attempt to do in this book is to illustrate how, as a manager, consultant, trainer, teacher or any other person interested in the development of people and organizations, you can use the portfolio approach to enhance your own work and therefore that of others. The examples I shall use will be real ones, showing different ways of using portfolios. They include a large firm of catering contractors, a county authority, a public sector business, a regional information charity and a national voluntary network. They will illustrate how a portfolio approach can be used to:

- improve business effectiveness;
- enhance the use of human resources;
- develop a team; and
- change training policy.

Within each of these organizational aims, the underpinning purpose of development for the individuals involved was essential.

What is a portfolio?

On the face of it, there seems no need to make a big song and dance about this question since a portfolio is simply a tangible record of what someone has done. It gets complicated only when limitations are imposed or when the evidence shown in the portfolio has to conform to particular and required standards of competence. Since, within the currently held view of what a portfolio is, both these points are normally true, we have to go beyond the simple description. Limitations have to be put on what goes into a portfolio, otherwise the contents would become too unwieldy. The selection of what is included must depend upon the needs and interests of the individual and on the purpose of the portfolio. The standards of competence required depend upon somebody deciding what they are, and somebody else interpreting what the standards mean and judging whether or not they have been attained through the provision of evidence in the portfolio. It does get a bit complicated then. It also runs the risk of becoming a sterile and counterproductive exercise unless great care is taken.

Another way to look at what a portfolio is, and the one that I shall be emphasizing, is to get back to basics. Even then, it is not enough to say that a portfolio is a record of what someone has done. The portfolio records five aspects, each of them demonstrating a stage of development, each of them requiring specific thought and attention. Above all, what I have discovered in the course of exploring the potential of portfolio-building as an approach, is the immense value that people as individuals, that teams in the workplace and that organizations as a whole can gain through the process itself. What's more, the beauty of using a portfolio approach is that it can be integrated into any personnel development process or training programme, giving it considerably added value.

The following are the five aspects recorded in portfolio-building:

1. *Experience:* This is **the story** of what happened, what was done, what was seen, what heard, what made, what written, what said.
2. *Learning:* This is the **discovery** that what happened has some significance for doing or changing things in the future.
3. *Demonstration:* This is the evidence or **proof** that shows that what has been learnt is actually used in the workplace or other relevant setting. This might be seen as the core of the portfolio, but it has to be accompanied by the other aspects if we are really interested in development.
4. *Learning needs:* This is **ownership**. It's when people take responsibility for what and how they develop.
5. *Learning opportunities:* Here we have the real marker for **growth** and the sign that change is taking place.

The five aspects of the portfolio:

- the story,
- discovery,
- proof,
- ownership, and
- growth,

constitute a development cycle, so that the last of these goes back into experience. From each growth point, in other words, comes another story. Later on, I shall describe the five aspects in more detail and illustrate them with a model and some practical examples.

Why is a portfolio helpful?

There are seven good reasons why portfolio-building is helpful:

- as a tool for self-development;

- to assess prior learning;
- to gain accreditation;
- to share good practice;
- to evaluate training;
- to enhance performance; and
- to change a culture.

The first three are the ones that are most usually recognized and accepted as the main purposes for building portfolios. In particular, the second and third are seen as the most valid reasons. This is to underrate the potential use of the portfolio approach and to underestimate its value.

The first on my list as a valid and valuable reason for portfolio-building is that it is a powerful tool for **self-development**. Tackled sensitively and professionally, assisting someone to build his or her own portfolio can have benefits far beyond the initial expectation of the process. I will go into the process for this, and the other six that follow, in some detail. For the moment, I'd ask you to consider some of the possible gains for you and your employees, trainees or clients of your instigating a process through which people regularly recognized their talents and reviewed how they could improve their performance.

The second, and the original, helpful purpose for building portfolios is to **assess prior learning**. I'd like to avoid much of the jargon that has the habit of creeping into anything that smacks of being new so that it appears to gain a credibility of its own. The assessment of prior learning, or APL, is one such piece of jargon. Portfolios were initially developed by colleges in the United States as a way of assisting mature students to gain credit exemptions for courses. The evidence people could give of previous experience and of aptitudes in relevant areas would be taken into account when negotiating which parts of the college programme were appropriate for the student. As a way in for anyone entering training or going on to further development, building a portfolio is an excellent indicator both for the learner and the trainer.

The third good and very solid use for a portfolio is that it is the ideal and healthy way to gain **accreditation**. The portfolio provides the evidence that someone can do something, not that he or she has been on a training course or passed an examination. When the portfolio shows sufficient evidence that the person has the competences required against a given set of standards, credits can be awarded by the relevant body. There is a philosophical distinction between purely competence-based assessment and portfolio learning. If that distinction is not made and understood, the portfolio will be in danger of becoming a checklist of skills at best, a tool for excluding people at worst. I shall be debating and illustrating the difference and the implications later.

Apart from those three important and helpful uses for portfolio-building, there are others of equal value that may have an even greater impact on the development of people and the organizations in which they work.

The first of those other ways is for portfolios to be used as a way of **sharing good practice**. The portfolio in this instance is a very different product. Portfolios vary, in any case, according to the use to which they are being put, as well as to the individuality of their owners. Where the purpose is for sharing good practice, the process as well as the product is quite different. I shall be sharing with you some good practice from some of the organizations that have worked in this way. The team development and the practical improvements that have accrued as a result have, in some cases, been quite remarkable.

The next extremely helpful use for a portfolio approach to learning is as an aid to **evaluating training**. Incorporated into any training programme, the development of people's portfolios is a continual guide to their performance and the effectiveness of the training. Training programmes can be the best place to introduce people to portfolio-building. The implications for trainers, for the design of the programmes and for the follow-up arrangements are considerable. I will be describing the practical application of portfolio work on training courses in some depth.

The sixth way that portfolio-building can be helpful, and probably the bottom line for most people, is that it can be seen to **enhance performance**. This is a case of the product being the process. What I mean by that is that the actual process of people developing portfolios almost invariably means that they develop their awareness of their own skills and shortcomings as well as their ideas on how to improve things. That very consciousness-raising activity leads to positive change by individuals, by teams and by organizations.

This takes us to the last and potentially the most dramatic of all the ways in which a portfolio approach can cause development. Used as part of a planned and cohesive development, that is to say with the active involvement of people at all levels within an organization, portfolios can help to **change a culture**. If portfolios are about self-development, assessing prior learning, accreditation, sharing good practice, evaluating training and enhancing performance, then when the processes I will be describing are put into place, a culture change is almost inevitable. If portfolios are seen only as a way to get qualified, the training revolution will have been a costly failure.

How portfolios link with the current training revolution

When I talk to people, and I include among them many trainers, about the training revolution, they often look at me as though I have just arrived from another planet, or at least as though I am being subversive. We are, nevertheless, in the midst of a totally different approach to training from that practised in the past. The difference between what is going on and most revolutions is that the change is being stimulated in Britain by changes in central policy rather than through a desire overtly expressed by people in the field. The consequence is that managers and trainers have been slow in recognizing the implications for them, or even that the changes have any significance for them at all.

Everywhere there is a growing awareness of the need for a better trained workforce, particularly in the sphere of management. Increasingly there is a recognition that the key attributes needed by people in a constantly changing work environment are:

* flexibility;
* self-motivation;
* communication skills; and
* a willingness and ability to develop new skills.

What there has not yet been is a conscious, cohesive effort to approach training – or education more generally – in a way that enables people to develop those attributes. Instead people have

been, and are still, trained in practical skills that may be of immediate use to them (if they have, or can find, a job that calls for those
skills). Even then the skills they gain may prove to be of very
transitory use if people don't have the ability to develop as the
needs of their jobs change because of new customer demands, tech-
nological developments or different working practices, or, indeed,
to make the best of prospects for promotion.

The training revolution bears the message, 'let's define the skills
and standards needed to carry out different jobs in order to ensure
quality of goods and service; then let's officially recognize that
people can do those jobs once they have demonstrated that they
have the required competences'. If that message is taken at face
value the effect can be quite sterile and limiting. People are asked
to produce profiles of their competence that are little more than
checklists in order to satisfy an assessor that certain activities have
been undertaken. There is little learning, scant attention is given
to quality or to personal development, and the task is seen as
laborious, time-wasting and bureaucratic.

When the underlying implications of the message are seen, the
training revolution really takes off. The process becomes productive and developmental. The message can then be expanded to say,
'let's enable people to discover their talents, to take responsibility
for their continuing development and to match their abilities to
the work they do now and can do in the future'. Furthermore, if we
use the portfolio approach in the way I shall describe, we can say,
'let's learn, as an organization, from the ideas and experiences of
our individuals and pool our resources more effectively in order to
improve the quality of our goods and services and ensure our own
development'.

The portfolio approach links in with those statements and concepts of the training revolution. It is a tangible, practical process
that works and has been proven to work, given the understanding,
commitment and skills of the managers and trainers who will be
carrying through and supporting the process. As the portfolio
approach is developed within organizations, the chances are high
that it will be seen as an important catalyst for growth rather than
simply as a way for individuals to gain qualifications.

The portfolio and qualifications

In Britain, National Vocational Qualifications (NVQs, or SVQs in Scotland) are the vehicle by which industries and professions can state competence requirements and through which individuals can gain accreditation. In management, the Management Charter Initiative (MCI) provides the basis for management accreditation. It is a different route from the acquisition of an MBA, although the two routes will undoubtedly come closer together. Many MBA programmes already have an element of portfolio development within them.

The statements of required competences that have been developed by Lead Bodies for the various specific industries and for generic management have provided the impetus for improving quality. The process of asking people to provide evidence of their prior learning in order to show what competences they bring with them is one step further down the quality route. The development of portfolios will be the third step towards continual improvement.

Qualifications are now being awarded on the basis of evidence that people can provide to show that they can achieve the relevant and required standards. It will no longer be sufficient to acquire theoretical knowledge. Practical evidence of ability in the workplace will be necessary. The question is, how can that evidence be provided? It would be clumsy and inefficient for people to go through a continual process of demonstrating everything they had to do before doing it. The answer is for people to build up their portfolios as they go along. Portfolios have so far mainly been used to accredit prior learning. That ignores the potentially developmental aspect of the approach. As people continue to do different things and gain new skills, to have ideas and experiment with new ways of doing things, they deserve to be recognized. Capturing these new skills and endeavours in the form of a portfolio will provide hard evidence of progress. The hard evidence can be gathered together, summarized as appropriate and used to gain further qualifications, promotion, new work or other rewards and recognition.

The fact that hardly anyone does this as a matter of course is because there has been little or no assistance. The processes described in this book are designed to help deal with that.

The gap in current practice and literature

Up to now, most of the literature on portfolio development has consisted either of a passing reference to 'people should present their portfolios of prior learning for assessment', or of a series of checklist-type questionnaires. Little has been written about the difficulties faced by people in developing their portfolios, or what kind of assistance can be given to them. Even less has been written about the potential of portfolio development for the benefit of teams and of organizations as a whole.

Charles Handy, in his book *The Age of Unreason*, has a chapter called 'Portfolio People' in which he presents the concept of people who gather together a range of skills and experiences in order to offer them to the marketplace, whether as paid or voluntary workers. His view that work will not be the same in the future as it has been in most of the twentieth century is not a new one. Eugene Heimler put forward a similar proposition in 1985 in his book *The Healing Echo*. Heimler didn't use the term 'portfolio' to describe his workforce of the future (now the present!) but rather saw that people would have a number of 'life-tasks' that would occupy their time in fulfilling ways.

In more technical terms, there have been a number of publications that have touched on portfolio development, most of which have been working papers, reports and brief guidelines. Some of these will be found in the reference section.

How to develop people through portfolio development

In Calgary, Canada, I met a man who sold hot-dogs. George had fled from Poland under the Communist regime, having survived a childhood under the Nazis. He had never known freedom until he came to Canada. In Poland he had been a doctor. Freedom in Canada had not extended to his being able to transfer his medical qualifications to practise in Calgary, so he opened a hot-dog stand. At first this seemed a waste of his talents, but as I watched him at work it became clear that he was doing much more than selling hot-dogs. He talked to people, philosophized with them, listened to them, laughed with them, gave them compliments. He probably spent the same amount of time with his customers as the average doctor (in Poland anyway) and probably provided them with more happiness, pause for thought and healing. He told me that, once he had overcome his ecstasy at being in a free country and his disappointment at being rejected as a doctor, he had decided that he could use his skills and carve out a very different 'practice' for himself in a place that offered the opportunity.

It's not everyone who could make such a startling transition. George showed that he had the necessary attributes to do so: flexibility, self-motivation, communication skills and a willingness and ability to develop new skills. I am certainly not suggesting that doctors would make good hot-dog vendors, or vice-versa! I do suggest that, if we look at the talents that people have and help them to express those talents, we will have a much more flexible and dynamic workforce.

The real and practical assistance that we can offer is to help people to develop their portfolios. The rest will follow, as I hope this book and your own good practice will illustrate.

Chapter 2

Portfolios for Personal Development

Personal development as a concept has received a mixed press over the past few years, mainly because it has been dealt with in so many different ways – ranging from Transcendental Meditation to hang-gliding from a Welsh mountainside. Portfolio-building as a way towards personal development is a process that encourages people to think about their attributes, to record and demonstrate to themselves and others what their qualities are, to take responsibility for their own continual learning, and to gain new skills and self-confidence.

When I first began to investigate ways of helping people to build their portfolios, I would ask them what they thought their strengths were. Almost invariably, they would tell me their weaknesses, or would say what they thought I wanted to hear within a narrow sphere of their particular area of work.

When looking at portfolios as a process for personal development, it is important not to start with the negative things nor to put constraints on the individual. Our aim is quite the opposite. Since most of us find it hard to avoid being subjective about our strengths and weaknesses, it is important to use neutral language. Rather than ask about strengths or qualities or competences at the start, therefore, we need to ask people about their experience before we can usefully get them to recognize what their qualities are. Our task is to encourage people to think as widely as possible about their attributes.

In order to do this it has been shown, ironically, that people need to have a structure to help them to think creatively and widely about themselves. The structure we provide is in the form of carefully formulated questions designed to take people through the five steps I have already described. Those steps are:

1. Describing **experience**: (a) **the index**; (b) **the story**.
2. Identifying **learning** from experience: **the discovery**.
3. The **demonstration** of practice: **the proof**.
4. Establishing **learning needs: ownership**.
5. Identifying and taking up **learning opportunities**: (a) **growth**; (b) **review**.

1(a) The index – describing experience

The starting point for portfolio development is the building of an index. This will be in a rough form at first. The aim of this is to begin to establish the *range* of experiences that a person has. For some people, this first stage is quite easy; others may need some guidance before they get the hang of it. The index may be seen as being in the form of 'chapter headings'. These are brief reminders of a whole range of things that someone has done, or events that have taken place that have some significance for the portfolio-builder.

In order to appreciate fully the potential impact for the development of individuals, I invite you to try out the processes described here, starting with the development of an index. You will need a note pad, or you might prefer to start compiling a more formal portfolio.

First, note down three experiences that have been of some significance to you. They may be to do with work, with your education and training, with your leisure-time activities, or with family or other life events. They may be recent experiences or something that you were involved with in the past. The only criterion is that the experience belongs to you. I suggest that you choose three different kinds of experience, say one from work, one from training and one from your personal life. All you are asked to do at this stage is to jot down three or four words on each as a reminder to you of what they are. Please do this now, before you read on, just to see what you come up with without looking at what others have written.

Experience 1

Experience 2

Experience 3

Here are some example of the things that people have included in their emerging index:

> being a team leader for the first time
> designing our new office layout
> going to my first interview
> conducting my first interview
> managing a soccer team
> the birth of my son
> the death of my father
> buying a house
> car-racing
> being made redundant
> getting my Open University degree
> running a training course for trainers

At first sight, it may appear that some of those experiences do not have much potential in terms of someone being able to demonstrate relevant competences. In fact, as I will show, they have all been the raw material for some compelling evidence and have given the individuals concerned some insights into their own abilities and how they can extend themselves.

The sample pro-forma in figure 2.1 gives space for 40 experiences; the more people can record, the better.

Simply giving the form to people for them to complete without assistance is likely to prove unproductive. What usually holds people back from recording their own experiences is that they are concerned about putting down the 'wrong' things. It is important to emphasize right from the start that:

- the portfolio will be their own property;
- what goes into the portfolio is entirely up to them (they may care to show only parts of it to someone else);

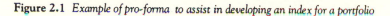

PORTFOLIO OF............................

INDEX OF EXPERIENCE to include any experience of significance to you from work, education, training, leisure interests, unpaid work, life events.

1	21
2	22
3	23
4	24
5	25

Figure 2.1 *Example of pro-forma to assist in developing an index for a portfolio*

- there cannot be any wrong things to include as long as they are recording experiences that belong to them;
- experiences themselves are neutral – they may have felt positive about some experiences and negative about others, but all are potential sources for learning; and
- as the person assisting, you will maintain a code of confidentiality and will provide the support needed for the individual to develop his or her portfolio for the purposes agreed.

If you need to give examples, do so, as long as these illustrate the breadth of experiences sought and neither limit nor intimidate the person. Sometimes a general discussion first can be helpful before asking him or her to commit anything to paper.

1(b) The story – describing experience

Once somebody has recalled a dozen or so experiences and recorded them in his or her index, there is likely to be a wide enough variety to begin the building of a portfolio in earnest and probably enough potential material to ensure a wealth of learning for the individual. The index can be added to at any time. In fact the development of a portfolio is a great encouragement to the person to continue to add new, or newly remembered, experiences as a way of recognizing personal strengths.

If the index is an indication of the *breadth* of someone's experience, the story is the indication of the *depth* of that experience. We are now seeking a more detailed description of the specific experiences outlined in the items in the index. Try this out for yourself before asking someone else to do it.

Look at the items you noted in the three experiences you recorded for your own portfolio (if you didn't do that before, this is a good time to go back to that section before carrying on). Select one of those items from your index. Now describe the experience, making it as specific as you can about a particular incident from the experience that stands out to you. For example, rather than just talk about the three years you spent as a deep-sea diver, talk about the time you came face-to-face with a great white shark. It will help if you think out loud, or better still, find a colleague prepared to listen to you for a few minutes.

When you have talked about the experience, write down a summary of what you have said in just a few lines. At this stage the summary is simply a brief description of the experience, but detailed enough to give anyone who reads it a clear picture of what you did or what happened. Use this, or a similar space elsewhere, for your summary.

Description of experience

What follows are some examples from experiences that people have described and summarized in their portfolios, taken from the index items noted on page 22. Each person has responded to the request to 'select one item from your index and describe the experience' and then to 'make a summary of what you have described and write it down'.

CASE STUDY 1

Description of experience

'When I was promoted to being team leader for the first time, I was

petrified that I'd get things wrong. I was worried that I couldn't ask any of the team for advice because I thought that they would ridicule me and not give me any respect in the future. I hadn't realized at the time that they would have provided me with a lot of support. It probably took about six months longer than it needed to get things really going with our project because it took so long for me to trust the team (and myself) well enough to share ideas around.'

CASE STUDY 2

Description of experience

'I had the job of redesigning our whole office layout. I was given a budget and control of the whole project. It was the first time that I'd been given the responsibility for a project from start to finish and it made me feel really motivated and delighted when I saw the end result and especially when others were pleased with the changes and congratulated me.'

CASE STUDY 3

Description of experience

'My first interview when I had just left school was with a man who sat behind an enormous desk in a vast office. I had to walk right across the room to get to him and he didn't get up. Then he fired questions at me and I couldn't think of anything to say. I didn't get the job.'

CASE STUDY 4

Description of experience

'The first time I conducted an interview, I was probably as nervous as the interviewee. I used the ideas I'd gained from a training course I had been on and video we'd seen. The practice from that gave me a good grounding and I did the preparation that I would never have done

otherwise. My manager, who was doing the interview with me, told
me afterwards it was the best interview he'd been involved in and
asked what the secret was.'

Note that at this point people have not been asked, nor have they
said, what they learnt from the experience. Nor have they been
asked to relate it to any competences required of them at this stage.
In order for people to get the most out of portfolio-building, a
carefully structured interview and sequence of questions is needed.
While the essence of portfolio development is simple, it is crucial
to remember that, for most people, this approach to learning is
quite new and will almost always require a step-by-step process.
The techniques described in this book have been used successfully
with hundreds of people over a seven-year period. The trainer or
manager with an appreciation of the underlying philosophy of the
approach and following the steps described will help others to
develop their portfolios, and therefore themselves, as successfully.

Here are some more summaries of descriptions of experiences
from the index list previously given:

CASE STUDY 5

Description of experience

'I managed a football team for three years. Once one guy broke his
leg; I heard it go! His brother was playing as well and was very
distressed. I called the ambulance and made sure that the injured
player and his brother were looked after and the family informed. The
team wanted to call the game off, but I persuaded them that they
should carry on, which they did. After that, they seemed to respect
me much more.'

In the above case, the person had initially seen his three-year stint
as manager of the football team as his experience. When pressed
for a specific experience, he chose to focus on this one incident
from which, as we shall see later, he was able to recognize and
demonstrate some of his qualities as a manager.

Some experiences are very personal and at first sight seem difficult to deal with. However, they can also be the most rewarding in

terms of the potential insights people can gain in being able to transform personal, and sometimes negative, experiences into something that they are able to learn from and use in entirely different circumstances.

CASE STUDY 6

Description of experience

'I was present with my wife at the birth of my son. It was the most amazing experience of my life.'

When asked what he had learned from the birth of his son, this young man, a junior manager in a large electronics industrial company, said 'not to have another one!' This surprising response looked as though it might draw a blank in terms of the rest of his portfolio, at least in relation to this particular experience, but it was to lead on to some even more surprising results, as you will see from the fuller account of the interview recounted later in this chapter.

CASE STUDY 7

Description of experience

'The experience that had the most effect on me in the past three years was the death of my father. I found myself the only one in the family who seemed able to deal with all the practical arrangements and also to help hold people together.'

CASE STUDY 8

Description of experience

'Going through the whole process of buying a house taught me a lot. I did my own negotiating, conveyancing, budgeting, surveying and

making the financial arrangements. I got it all from books. Now other people come to me for advice.'

CASE STUDY 9

Description of experience

'I race cars in my spare time. I have to manage the whole thing; all the safety aspects, the entrance forms and all the administration. If I don't do things properly and check everything meticulously, I could get killed.'

The people who presented these as experiences were junior or aspiring managers. They had not been given, nor taken, any real degree of responsibility in their work; in fact, all three had expressed reservations about their ability to take on management roles. Yet their life or spare-time experience began to show the levels to which they could all aspire given the situation and the motivation. None of these people's managers had any inkling of the three experiences described, nor therefore of the potential managerial competences of their staff.

CASE STUDY 10

Description of experience

'I was made redundant from my last job a year ago. It was a real blow to me and it made me see things quite differently. I'd imagined that I had a safe job for life. After that I realized that things can change at any time and that I could actually deal with the insecurity better than I had imagined.'

CASE STUDY 11

Description of experience

'Getting my degree through the Open University was quite an achievement for me. I had spent seven years of part-time study,

having started with no qualifications or academic study at all for over fifteen years. Getting the degree showed me that I could do something that I had previously thought impossible.'

CASE STUDY 12

Description of experience

'I designed and ran a training course for trainers. Most of them were fairly new to training, but others were quite experienced, so it was a real challenge. I was able to use the experience of some of the participants productively in the end, although at first I was anxious about being swamped by them.'

The last three experiences can give indications of practical skills being obtained, but mostly what these people are showing are changes in understanding and attitudes. Those are notoriously the most difficult things to show within somebody's portfolio, yet many of the competences required, particularly within management and in the personal care professions, are intangible. We shall explore how the portfolio development process can assist with the intangible as well as the practical skills that people need to demonstrate.

2. The discovery – identifying learning from experience

Once people have begun to identify their experience, they will be ready for the next step. As you work with this process you will almost certainly recognize the varying degrees to which people are able to conceptualize what is going on and how they can get to grips with the structure you are providing. What you will also almost certainly recognize is the importance of having that structure, without which people are likely to flounder and wander about aimlessly.

This next main step is for the portfolio-builder to explore what he or she has learnt from the experience that has just been summarized. In order to get to that, you will first need to ensure that:

(a) the person has recorded the experience in summary form; and (b) that this experience is sufficiently specific to be of value. Once again, the best way of testing this out is to try it yourself first. Look back at the summary you have made of your own selected experience. Now consider what you have learnt from it. As before, ideally discuss it with a colleague, or at least think it through out loud yourself; then write down a summary here.

What I learnt from this experience

Translating an experience into learning can be quite difficult. Few people are asked to think about what they have done and what they learnt from it. The result is that we tend to devalue our knowledge and experience and not share it with others. This part of the portfolio process is intended to encourage the start of a continuing cycle of development. It is not until people begin to recognize that they can learn from almost any event in their lives that we shall see any real change in the way things happen.

Once again, the learning can be related or apparently quite unrelated to the actual work someone is doing or to the stated competences that are required. The learning may also be stated in tangible and concrete ways, like a new skill gained, or in intangible ways, such as changes in perception or understanding. At this stage, in order to encourage the creative development of people and their portfolios, it is important to allow, even stimulate, the widest range of thoughts that people have about what they have learnt from a particular event or experience. Remember that this is about *discovery*. Pinning the discovery down to something more relevant and tangible, if necessary, comes at the next stage.

Here are some of the responses to questions about what people have learnt from their experiences, drawing on the same examples as before. Rather than go through all twelve, I have selected four of the experiences previously described: numbers 1, 5, 6 and 10. In each case, I will repeat the experience as summarized and go on to record the responses to the question 'what did you learn from this?'

CASE STUDY 1 'Caroline'

Description of experience

'When I was promoted to being team leader for the first time, I was petrified that I'd get things wrong. I was worried that I couldn't ask any of the team for advice because I thought that they would ridicule me and not give me any respect in the future. I hadn't realized at the time that they would have provided me with a lot of support. It probably took about six months longer than it needed to get things really going with our project because it took so long for me to trust the team (and myself) well enough to share ideas around.'

What I learnt from this

'I learnt to trust people more and to expect the best of them. I also learnt to consult more with colleagues and to ask questions and share ideas. I think I've also learnt to have more confidence in myself.'

This woman was working with a relatively new team in a rapidly changing and highly competitive environment where getting new projects off the ground quickly was crucial. She had not seen herself as a manager before being invited to take on her current post and had felt isolated and unsupported. Only when she began to build her portfolio did she see how she had developed and what she could now offer.

CASE STUDY 5 'Derek'

Description of experience

'I managed a football team for three years. Once one guy broke his leg; I heard it go! His brother was playing as well and was very distressed. I called the ambulance and made sure that the injured player and his brother were looked after and the family informed. The team wanted to call the game off, but I persuaded them that they should carry on, which they did. After that, they seemed to respect me much more.'

What I learnt from this

'From this, I learnt that I could take decisions in a crisis and take the necessary action. I learnt that I could persuade people to do things even when they didn't want to do them; and that I can gain the respect of people when I take a clear and strong line.'

In the above two instances, the managers who presented their examples were able to generalize about what they had learnt from their respective experiences and could make quite easy transitions from their stories to what they had discovered about themselves and what they could do. They needed little prompting to do this, although the second of these two people was finding it hard to see how he put this into practice in the workplace. This would not become clear to him until we went on to the next part of the process.

The next example was rather different. He had already related a very profound and personal experience as the one he wanted to talk about, although he found it hard to express himself.

Case study 6 'Clyde'

Description of experience

'I was present with my wife at the birth of my son. It was the most amazing experience of my life.'

What I learnt from this

'I learnt not to have any more children!'

Since the two statements were in such conflict with each other, it was necessary to ask some further questions to clarify what he meant. Sometimes people will make apparently unconnected statements about what they have experienced and what they have learnt. Part of the developmental process of portfolio-building is to help people see the connection between doing and learning, and then between learning and the application of that learning. In this case, I asked Clyde what made him say that he'd learnt not to have any more children. Following this part of our conversation, which took about ten minutes, I asked him to summarize what he'd said and to write it down.

'After all the excitement I came down to hard reality. It meant we couldn't go out and had to be careful about what we spent. I learnt about the real value of money, and what the important things really were. Most of all, I've learnt to be responsible for my own actions for the first time and to accept responsibility for someone who is dependent upon me. And I hope I've learnt to think ahead about the implications of my actions.'

It was not easy for this young man to make sense of what he had learnt and to write it down. He needed constant reminders of what he had said and he had to be prompted to write down his summaries. Yet when he had done this he sat back, read what he had written and remarked that he now felt more positive about himself than he had felt since the actual experience of his son's birth. The key word for him had been 'responsibility', something he had apparently never recognized before in himself. In the light of his relatively new role as a manager, together with his apparent reluctance in this role, this was a pretty significant discovery.

CASE STUDY 10 'Martin'

Description of experience

'I was made redundant from my last job a year ago. It was a real blow to me and it made me see things quite differently. Before I imagined that I had a safe job for life. After that I realized that things can change at any time and that I could actually deal with the insecurity better than I had imagined.'

What I learnt from this

'Now that I look back on this, I see that I have changed quite a bit. I *learnt to take risks and to take new ideas on board without always rejecting them out of hand as I probably would have done in the past.'*

This manager was a relative newcomer to the company he worked for and had come in at a time of great and inevitable change which was being resisted by many of his colleagues. He was able to see the benefits of his previous negative experience in the light of his current situation and how this would help him to deal with the new circumstances. It was by stopping and thinking about his experience and what he had learnt that he was able to recognize later on how he could help others to be more positive about impending changes.

3. The proof – demonstrating practice

The essence of the portfolio is not experience, nor even what has been learnt from that experience. It's evidence of good practice, or proof that someone can actually do something that he or she claims to be able to do. When the focus is on personal development, the key factor is the recognition by the individual portfolio-builder that he or she has a range of personal and technical qualities and can prove it.

Arriving at the proof may often entail a creative leap or two of the imagination – in itself an important quality. In helping others to do this, you will again see the difference in pace and abilities of the people developing their portfolios. Learning theorists such as David Kolb propose that people learn in different ways and that this may make it difficult if not impossible for some people to conceptualize, for example, and make generalizations from specific experiences. My own work on portfolio development indicates that while people do have different preferences and abilities, almost everyone is able to go round the Portfolio Learning Cycle of the five stages that I have already briefly described.

The only real difference is the level of support that people will need at any of the five stages. Practically everyone will need guidance at first; most people will require less and less as they go on. Some will need considerable support even to describe their experiences, others to reflect on what they have learnt. Very few people will not need some initial encouragement to write down, or record in some other way, their own summaries, although the helper must always ensure that the portfolio-builder does take on that responsibility for him or herself.

For the first few occasions, help is most likely to be required at the stage of giving the proof. As before, therefore, it might be helpful if you can find someone you can rely on to ask you the right questions, which should be both challenging and supportive, to help you to think through and record what evidence you have that proves you have learnt what you have said you have learnt.

From your previous recordings, consider now how you use what you have learnt from the specific experience you selected within your own work or other activity. This may mean putting what you have learnt into a different context from the original experience, or it may mean bringing it up to date, or it may mean recognizing that you don't actually use what you have learnt, or use it in a different or unexpected way. In any event, record the summary of what you discuss or think about here; then consider the practical supporting evidence you could find to provide the actual proof of the quality of this bit of your work or other activity.

How I can demonstrate that I use what I've learnt from this experience

The supporting evidence I can attach to my portfolio includes:
(eg photos, certificates, letters, reports, tapes, notes, minutes, designs, proposals, budgets etc)

From the examples given, here are the summaries recorded by the portfolio-builders after the interviews I had with them. These are their responses to the question 'how can you demonstrate that you use what you've learnt now?'

Case study 1 'Caroline'

How I can demonstrate that I use what I've learnt and give supporting evidence

'*Two months ago I was asked to lead a project team to draw up plans for a new proposal we have been asked to tender for. I got the team together and we started by having a brain-storming session. This stimulated a lot of ideas and enthusiasm, mainly because it was a different way of working for most of them. The end result was that we came up with a good plan and a lot of commitment from the team to go forward with the proposal. I never had the confidence to work with the team this way before.*'

I asked the manager to say what she could show in some tangible form to prove that she had the qualities she claimed she had gained.

'*I can show the plans we drew up. I have a copy of the notes from the brain-storming session that show all the ideas. I'll include the timetable for the latest project and I can compare this with the previous programme that took far longer to complete. I could get some feedback from members of the team; perhaps give them a questionnaire to say how they assess my performance; and my manager has already complimented me; I will ask him to put it in writing. And if we succeed in getting our tender accepted, I'll frame the contract.*'

It took some time before this woman began to see what she could include as tangible proof of her growing confidence and ability. Once she started, she saw a range of possibilities. And as she talked and made her summary, she seemed to grow even more in confidence.

Case study 5 'Derek'

How I can demonstrate that I use what I've learnt and give supporting evidence

'*I don't think I really do this in my work. I haven't been given the opportunity, or I haven't taken it. I can see that there are things I could have done but as yet I haven't been in a position where I have taken the lead or attempted to influence others. I can now see that I could do this. I'm not sure how to yet. As far as managing the football team is concerned, I could certainly show some letters and awards for the work I did with the team and I'm sure that they'd write some kind of testimonial for the incident and how I handled it.'*

Here is an example of some real potential development. This was a recently promoted manager who was not yet managing, having had little or no training or preparation for the job, in an organization strong on hierarchy but weak on management. He had, perhaps for the first time, recognized that he had a management skill that he should and could be using in his work. He was not yet able to demonstrate the skill within the workplace. The potential for his development was clear; if he could find a way to practise those skills within the work setting he would enhance his own competences and improve the way he managed himself and other people. The next two steps in the portfolio process would help to take him forward.

CASE STUDY 6 'Clyde'

How I can demonstrate that I use what I've learnt and give supporting evidence

'I do take more responsibility at work now. I take much more care in ordering equipment and in making out a case for what I see to be the most cost-effective, safe and efficient way of carrying out a new testing procedure, for example. The other thing I do now is to listen to my staff more and help them to plan their workload better. And I always ask if what they suggest is realistic and to let me know what they think the consequences will be of doing something in a particular way. I can put into my portfolio some of my more recent proposals and budgets for equipment, with the options I've given. I could ask some of my staff if they would mind my including some of their work plans with comments about how my input has helped them. Our finance manager would let me have a note about savings I have helped to achieve over the past year without any loss in quality.'

This young manager had initially found it hard to make any sense of what he could put into his portfolio and had struggled to think of experiences to put into his index. What he was now able to articulate was a far cry from the experience he had selected – ie the birth of his son. Yet for him it had been a starting point and this helped him to take more ownership of his own qualities. He was also able to see how he could connect a personal experience with how he used the competences gained within his work environment. The key word for him was 'responsibility' and this would take him further as he went on with his portfolio.

CASE STUDY 10 'Martin'

How I can demonstrate that I use what I've learnt and give supporting evidence

'I can demonstrate this just by the way I am now, at work and personally. I'm much more relaxed than I used to be and more able to handle other people's negativity and grumbles without it getting to me. I also take a longer term view of things in a positive light even if they entail big changes. In fact I am more inclined to welcome the idea of change now and to plan for the outcomes of that change rather than hide my head or sit back and wait as I used to. As far as being able to provide proof, I can show a paper I've written proposing how we might plan for the impending changes in our structure and a letter from our director who was very supportive after I presented the paper at a staff conference. I would ask some of my staff for their written, or maybe taped, comments about my style in dealing with change. Probably the most significant piece of evidence is the fact that almost all of my staff now seem much more positive than they were about changes, even though they are uncertain about their own futures. I can ask them specific questions on that and record their responses. My wife would probably be the best person to comment on my state of health and temper these days.'

4. Ownership – establishing learning needs

Proving one's own abilities, or demonstrating competences, may be the central point and part of building a portfolio, but in terms of personal development it can only be half of the process. In the past, training and the gaining of professional qualifications has been regarded as an end in itself. Gaining the certificate or diploma, or attending the training course, has been sufficient to satisfy learners and teachers alike that competence has been achieved. Leaving school, finishing university, completing that training course was the goal. Then we didn't have to learn any more.

Hand in hand with that approach to learning went the concept that education and training was something that someone else wanted us to go through. The messages were, and often still are: 'if you want to get a good job, you'll have to get a qualification' or 'you need to improve your communication skills; there's a course coming up that you should go on', or 'if you're thinking of promotion, how about that finance skills seminar?'. Increasingly, the move is towards continual learning, and towards the individual taking responsibility for his or her own development.

There are two main difficulties in people taking responsibility for and ownership of their own learning. The first is that, particularly in larger, more traditional organizations, this has not been encouraged. Where training has been offered, it has been on the basis of spoon-feeding. The second difficulty is that it is hard to define one's own learning needs without support. The portfolio approach can give the support required for personal development through its structure, through the backing of individuals and organizations, and because it is a continual process.

Having provided the proof that you are able to do something, or have a particular quality, I am now going to ask you to consider what it is that you need to improve on within the area that you have selected. Look back at the recordings you have made so far and when you have thought about the question, write down your summary.

What I still need to improve in this area

The chances are fairly high that, no matter how experienced and competent you are in your work, you will be able to identify something that you feel you could improve. In fact, the more competent people are, the more likely it is that they will want to improve and develop themselves. Recently I saw the comment in a respected management development publication that 'someone who has an MBA may not always be right, but he's (*sic*) never in doubt'. That, if it were true, seems to me to be a startling condemnation of the results of training rather than, presumably (since it was in an advertisement for a college offering MBAs), praise of them.

The objectives of this step in the portfolio process are to encourage people to:

1. define for themselves what they still need to learn and to develop;
2. see that what they need to improve is relevant to them and their work or interests; and
3. accept responsibility for and ownership of their own learning.

Here are the responses to the question 'what do you still need to improve in this area' from our four case studies.

CASE STUDY 1 'Caroline'

What I still need to improve in this area

'Having begun to work with teams in this way, I see that I could do more. I need to gain some skills in working with a group; to get some more discipline in our discussion and arriving at decisions. Two things in particular: one is running meetings better, the other is getting the information into a better order so as to arrive at the best conclusions. The second part seems to be about analysing and planning, but being able to do that on the spot and with the team rather than after the meeting on my own.'

This manager now seemed to have gained sufficient confidence in her own skills to be able to recognize and accept fairly clearly what she needed to develop in herself. She was doing this in a positive light; rather than 'I can't do this', it was 'I can do more'. She had still needed to discuss this and to spend a little time thinking back through what she had said and recorded earlier before coming to this conclusion, but once she got there she was committed to the idea.

Case study 5 'Derek'

What I still need to improve in this area

'I've got to use the skills I have. I don't think the people I supervise respect me very much, perhaps because I want to be one of them too much. I need to lead them more and to act more decisively. What I need to develop is my leadership skills at work.'

Case study 6 'Clyde'

What I still need to improve in this area

'I need to see things in a more positive light. I tend to get bogged down by difficult things. The excitement of having a baby got dragged down by all the problems afterwards and I even took this into work. I didn't like having the responsibility at home or as a manager at work. I need to stop whining about things and start seeing that I can actually achieve things.'

The above two responses show a change in attitude taking place simply as a result of the reflection process that they were both going through. The latter seems as yet unclear as to what he actually has to do or how he might go about it, but this will be assisted by the next step in the process.

Case study 10 'Martin'

What I still need to improve in this area

'I think I may have become a bit too complacent about being able to

deal with change. I probably don't take into account the way other people are feeling. I will have a better idea if I ask my staff more specific questions. I think I need to listen to them more and help them to handle their worries rather than brush them aside. I'm not sure how to do that.'

5(a) Growth – identifying and taking up learning opportunities

The fifth main step in the portfolio learning process is to establish a planned learning contract. The portfolio is not a historical record of achievement, nor even a current profile of competence. It is a living, growing collection of evidence that mirrors the growth of its owner, including his or her hopes and plans. In other words, the portfolio, like the person, is as much about the future as it is about the past and the present.

This stage is also about translating sometimes vague aspirations into more concrete actions. As such, once again, the portfolio-builder is likely to need assistance in thinking through the possibilities and opportunities. As the manager, trainer or mentor, you may well have access to information and resources that the learner could find useful. Or you may have knowledge about other potential opportunities within the organization or perhaps another part of your network.

Since this is the time for establishing a learning contract, you will also need to be assisting the learner to keep a broad view of what his or her learning opportunities are. They will include training courses with or without qualifications offered; but mainly they will include trying out new skills within the work environment, brief secondments to other managers or departments, having individual tutorials or consultancy assistance, visits to other sections, going to conferences and seminars, reading appropriate publications, or any of a myriad of other opportunities depending upon the need and the resources available.

As always, we need to ask the right questions at the right time. The one that is relevant now is 'how are you going to gain the additional competences you have identified that you need, and by when?' In preparation for helping someone else with this, try doing it for yourself now, following on from your previous responses.

How I'm going to gain the additional competences, and by when

You might also find it useful to go back to the two other items you put on your initial index and go through the whole process at this point; or you may prefer to practise on a colleague.

Here are the learning contracts established by the four people in our case studies.

CASE STUDY 1 'Caroline'

How I'm going to gain the additional competences, and by when

'I will talk to our training manager to see what courses are available on meetings skills. If there is nothing soon, I'll get hold of one of the videos that I'm sure we have access to or at least find something to read. Apart from that, I need to get some more practical experience. I will discuss with my own manager ways in which I could chair some of the other meetings that he currently runs, or at least co-chair some with him. I will concentrate on the things I need to improve, getting more order into the decision-making and being able to analyse the information. I'll draw up some kind of "before and after" chart so that I can judge how I'm doing. I'll talk to our training manager and my line manager next week and set up a timetable so that I've done what I want to do in three months' time.'

The above summary was made after quite a bit of thought and discussion. It is often quite difficult for people to translate their often unclear or general ideas about what they need to improve into the practical realities of what to do about it. In this case, it was even more important for Caroline to make the decision and take action based on her analysis, since this was just what she had said she wanted to do. So the process of portfolio-building was, for her, a skills development exercise in itself.

CASE STUDY 5 'Derek'

How I'm going to gain the additional competences, and by when

'*I'm going to decide first of all what our goals are over the next six months in our team. I'll need to talk to my manager about this and get some clear guidelines from him. I've never checked what our priorities are, so we always seem to work on an ad hoc basis. Then I will get my team together and brief them on what we need to be doing. I'll have a regular team meeting, probably once a month, to discuss progress and see whether we should be doing anything differently. I think if I see it as a football team I'll be able to manage the team better. I'll talk to my boss over the next few days and call my first team meeting in two weeks at the latest. I will also see if there are any leadership courses I could go on. I'm sure my boss gets that information, so I'll ask him about that as well.*'

The chances are high that Derek will discover two main things: first that, this not being a football team, things may not work quite as smoothly as he appears to imagine; and therefore second, that he needs to identify and gain some more specific skills, such as negotiating, planning, being assertive etc. It is very common that once people start to try out new things they discover others that they need and want to improve. This is, indeed, growth.

CASE STUDY 6 'Clyde'

How I'm going to gain the additional competences, and by when

'*It has been hard to see what I can do. With help, I have identified two things. I will make some practical changes to the office layout to improve the conditions that we're currently working under. People, including me, have been complaining about this for ages. There is no reason I can't get on and do something. I will draw up some proposals next week and discuss them with the others, then put the changes into effect, hopefully by the end of next month. The other thing for me to do is to find someone to sit down with on a regular basis to review how I'm doing. My boss doesn't do this with me. I'm not sure he's the right person anyway, but there's someone in the next section who would be helpful. I'll ask him to assist me in continuing my portfolio. I will see him tomorrow and will explain what we have been doing. He may even be interested in doing a portfolio himself and I could offer to help him.'*

Clyde had little confidence in his own manager, which may have reflected some of his own lack of self-confidence. He had, however, accepted some responsibility for getting on with things and for finding his own support, even giving support to a colleague. As with everyone, Clyde will need to review how he has carried out his plan for learning and there needs to be a structure for this as with all the other steps in the process. This will come in the second part of this stage.

CASE STUDY 10 'Martin'

How I'm going to gain the additional competences, and by when

'I remember in my previous job, the staff were just brought into the conference room and told that there were going to be redundancies because of the changing structure of the company. We were all left in a state of shock. I know I didn't perform well in my last three months there. Now that we are going through big changes here, and there may be some redundancies, although I think this will be minimal and through natural wastage, I want to make sure that my staff don't feel themselves in the same position as I did. I will make some time over the next few weeks to talk with each of them individually and listen to what they have to say as well as give them my own views about the future. I know I'm not a very good listener. At my last appraisal, my manager suggested I go on a counselling course and I think I now

understand why. I will ask him what he had in mind and see what our training centre is running in the near future.'

There seems to be quite a change in attitude here. Martin has accepted that he needs to listen more and that he has insufficient skills in this area, whereas from his last appraisal he does not appear to have taken this on board. The difference is probably at least in part because the portfolio process has enabled him to think about his own prior experience, and therefore some of his strengths, and then to reflect on where he wants to use that experience to improve what he already does. Someone who doesn't listen is not likely to listen to somebody telling him he doesn't listen! Working through it himself in his own way, within the structure of the portfolio, Martin arrived at his own conclusions and set his own learning contract. Next, he will have to look at whether or not he has gained better listening skills and is using them productively.

5(b) Review – identifying and taking up learning opportunities

This takes us on to the stage of the portfolio process that will test whether or not things are actually changing. Up until the end of the last stage, apart from the gathering together of substantiating evidence to prove what the portfolio-builder can do, the process has entailed only thinking, talking and recording. Between the last stage and this one, there has to have been some practical activity in the workplace or elsewhere, perhaps on a training programme. The plan for the activity has already been recorded. There may be a number of activities, depending on the extent to which the learner has been developing his or her portfolio and the number of learning needs and opportunities that have been identified. The length of time that is needed to carry out those activities will vary considerably; some tasks might be undertaken within a day or two, others could take several months to complete.

Development is seen to have taken place when there is some evidence that is has. The portfolio approach enables that to hap-pen by ensuring that there is a procedure for reviewing the results of any learning activity. Note that it is the *result* of the learning activity not the learning process itself that is important. Portfolios are concerned with evidence of good practice, whether the main objective is personal, professional, team or organizational development.

In the case of personal development, when the individual can see tangible evidence of his or her own achievements this will almost always raise confidence, enthusiasm, self-esteem and a desire to take things further. Good management practice will ensure that this happens within organizations. As we know, such good management practice is rare. Portfolio development will enhance the work of good management practitioners and assist other managers to gain new skills if they follow the structures described in this book.

The question to ask at this point is 'how have you gained the additional competences that you were seeking?' It needs to be asked at the appropriate and agreed time; that is to say, a short while after the activity or activities are to have been undertaken by the portfolio-builder.

The chances are that you have not yet had the time to do what you planned to do since you completed the last step yourself. If you have, you could complete this part now; otherwise you might like to come back to it later, just to check out the process.

Date:
How I gained the additional competence/s

When you have completed your summary for this section, you will see that you could now add this to your index and your story. In other words, the process is one of continual development; from the learning opportunities and activities taken up you have new experiences and competences to add to your portfolio. What's more, the developmental process is undertaken on a more conscious level so that self-awareness is built into the whole system – an essential factor in personal development.

We will take a final look at the people portrayed in the case studies to see how they used the process and reviewed their learning.

Case study 1 'Caroline'

Date: (Three months later)

How I gained the additional competence/s

'It took a bit longer than I thought. I finally managed to get on to a training course on meetings last week which was really helpful and gave me a lot of practice and ideas about where I can improve things. Mostly, it confirmed that what I've been doing over the past three months has been quite good. I did a checklist for myself of what I want to be achieving at my meetings. I have put that into my portfolio. This helped me to get a proper agenda and keep to the topics better. Several people have commented on how the meetings have improved and it showed at our last one when we got through some very tricky decisions that we needed to make. My manager was very supportive and encouraged me to get involved in other meetings, and even asked me to chair a new quality team meeting where most people were senior to me. It was quite nerve-racking but it went very well and I got several congratulations.'

Case study 5 'Derek'

Date: (one month later)

How I gained the additional competence/s

'We had a team meeting and I talked about my ideas for a regular session where we planned and reviewed our work. A few of them asked what it was all about and seemed to think I was going to have a go at them, but by the end they seemed to think it was a good idea. I didn't get a very clear idea from my boss about our priorities, but he did ask me to make my own suggestions. I gave them to him and he agreed with most of them but added a couple of things. When I talked to the team they thought we were being asked to do too much in the time. It was hard to get the team to make any positive suggestions. I fixed another date and spoke to my boss again. He promised to look at the workload and our resources and also to let me have information

*about training on leadership skills. I will follow this up in a day or two.
I realize from this that I still need to get better at leadership, but I feel
I have really started.'*

CASE STUDY 6 'Clyde'

Date: (two months later)

How I gained the additional competence/s

*'The office looks great and everyone seems really happy with it. We
just did some simple things, like moving the drawing boards to the
other side of the room where there is far more natural light and shifting
some of the computers to make them more accessible. We also gave
each person more space by the way we moved the desks and got rid of
some of the bookshelves and filing cabinets that didn't need to be in
our office. My boss came in as we were doing this to find out what
was going on. He was not pleased, but he calmed down after I
explained what we were doing. I should have discussed it with him
first. After that he suggested that we had a talk. He offered to help me
with my portfolio in the future and we fixed a date for next week.'*

CASE STUDY 10 'Martin'

Date: (six weeks later)

How I gained the additional competence/s

*'There wasn't a counselling course available that I could get on soon,
but we found a general two-day communication skills course that
includes listening skills. I'm booked on that in a couple of weeks' time.
Meanwhile I have met with all of my staff and spent at least half an
hour with each of them. I discovered that there is a lot of anxiety and
frustration and that people are not feeling very motivated to put their
best into things. I was really surprised. I believe that I have put their
minds at rest a bit and have arranged a further session with each of
them; in fact I have already met again with four of the twelve and they*

seem to be distinctly happier and have shown this in their work output over the past few weeks. I will continue to have regular meetings, although not necessarily individually, and intend to monitor how they are reacting to the changes taking place and listen to their ideas and concerns.'

As a personal development tool, the portfolio approach seems to be working for these people. We have only looked at the start of the process, since to see continuing development we would have to go through it several times and over a period of at least six months.

The procedure just described takes some time and of course is variable depending upon the person and the circumstances. Portfolio development is not a short cut to training, but it is almost certainly a cost-effective and productive way of encouraging people to gain new and relevant skills and understanding. It also speeds up. At first it may take up to an hour for an individual to think through and summarize, with the help of a mentor, the competences gained and learning needs identified from just one experience.

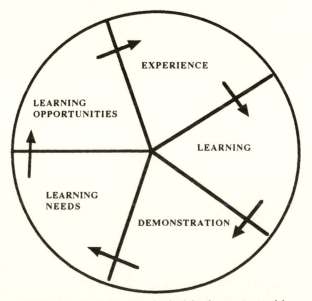

Figure 2.2 *Portfolios for individual development: a model*

Chapter 3

Portfolios for Professional Development

The difference between portfolios for personal development and portfolios for professional development lies not so much in the process but in the application. This chapter will illustrate how, in two different settings, people have gone about developing portfolios for their own professional or vocational advancement.

The training revolution has been brought about through the process of establishing universal sets of competence statements for a vast range of professions and vocations and, within them, for the specific roles and tasks to be carried out. Lead bodies have been established for most industries and many professions within Britain. Even where competence requirements have not been established, increasing numbers of companies and organizations are working towards writing their own required competences.

These are welcome moves. Quality standards are being set and translated into the practical, actionable tasks expected of people who are employed to carry out work to those standards. This is a culmination of the changes that have been taking place over the past few years. In the early part of the 1980s there was a move towards defining values and goals and putting those into mission statements. Later, there was a drive towards quality. In the early part of the '90s the talk and the work has been on competences. As we move towards the middle part of the decade, there will be a need to look at portfolios as the way towards achieving what has been a gradual drive towards greater success. That success can be summed up by the enhanced satisfaction of consumers, staff and investors in the goods and services offered, whether the business is making cars or providing health care.

The two settings that I shall now describe are a Management Development Centre working with British Rail and the Leisure Services Departments of two Local Government Authorities.

CASE STUDY 1

Developing portfolios within a management training programme

The Grove is a Management Development Centre offering training and consultancy to managers at its Watford base or tailor-made to clients' requirements at their own location. Historically, The Grove has provided training for managers in the railway industry, and this still accounts for the major part of its work.

British Rail was among the first industries to become involved in quality initiatives and in the emerging Management Charter Initiative. The Grove responded by using the competence statements as markers for its training objectives for specific programmes and by initiating a series of management training programmes that encouraged the development of portfolios by the participants. The programme was called 'The Developing Manager'.

Setting a contract

The Grove's client was one of the British Rail businesses which had recently started on the path towards privatization and had been engaged in a series of major structural and cultural changes within its management. The Grove had been asked to run a programme for a group of junior managers with the aim of helping them towards gaining the competences required.

The proposal made by The Grove included the content of the initial one-week programme, preparatory work and follow-up, and also portfolio development as an integral part of the work. Some time was taken to describe the portfolio process and its implications, particularly in terms of the follow-up required within the workplace. It was regarded as important by The Grove, in assisting their client to work towards the culture change required, that the training programme was not seen as a one-off event, but rather that there would be a continuation of competence development. This would be attained through the introduction of a portfolio approach, linked to MCI competences, with the supportive commitment of management throughout the organization. The contract was agreed.

Portfolio – a new concept

Despite a forward-looking senior management team and a commitment to NVQ and MCI competences, there was little understanding of what portfolios were or how they could be used to develop staff. This has been the case with all the organizations I have worked with over the past few years. In fact, British Rail management probably had a better grasp of the concept than most others at that time.

Working towards NVQs/MCI

The preparatory work that The Grove asked intending participants of this initial programme to undertake was in line with the MCI competence statements. Each person was given an assessment profile to discuss with his or her line manager. The profile began with a brief explanation and then asked the key questions that related to the MCI key competences. The questions were organized into the four main areas, or key roles of management:

- managing operations;
- managing finance;
- managing people; and
- managing information.

Each of those areas was sub-divided into a total of nine units, each of which was further sub-divided into the 26 elements that make up the level 1 MCI competences. Participants were asked to spend about an hour with their line managers making a joint assessment of their level of experience and competence relating to each of the elements. This was the first time that most of the participants or their managers had come across the required competences. Most participants reported that it had been a difficult exercise but that the discussions had been productive.

A topic-based training programme

The initial residential training programme for 'The Developing Manager' was designed largely as a traditional, workshop-based series of topics according to the expressed needs of the client. They included such things as interviewing skills, communication, motivation and time management. Each topic involved some input from the tutors but mainly consisted of practical experiential work with feedback.

Introducing portfolio

The idea of portfolio development was introduced during the opening session on the first day. Participants were often bemused at first, although some picked up the notion with alacrity and saw it as a practical way for them to record and gain credit for their past and current experience.

In introducing the notion of portfolio development, it is worth remembering that this is likely to be a new and apparently difficult learning process for most people, however simple it may appear to be when we are familiar with it and describe it to others. Fifteen of these programmes were run involving over 200 people and all but a handful found it hard to see how to go about building their portfolio until they had a chance to try it out. There were concerns about what was expected of them, what kind of experiences they could record and how they would do this, how much they would have to get through in the time allocated during the week, who would be looking at their work and so on.

Compiling an index

At the end of the first day, participants were asked to begin to note down some of their prior experiences. This was an individual task, which they were invited to share within their own learning sets of three or four people. This also proved difficult for most people. There was a diffidence towards committing anything of their own experience to paper at this stage, mainly because of the concern 'is this what is wanted?', which underlines the traditional approach to most of our training and education.

A daily diary

What people found easier was the request for them to complete a diary sheet at the end of each day. This asked them to describe the topics that had been covered, the ways in which they had engaged themselves in any activity, their key learning points, how they could use what they had learnt in their work and what, from this, they could include in their portfolio.

This was easier because it was more familiar, more immediate and more specific, with clear guidelines and an objective, which was that the learning sets would share their learning points and prepare a brief presentation of these for the following morning. Until the participants had seen and tried out portfolio work for themselves, they needed this kind of structure. On the other hand, until they had faced the blockages they imposed upon themselves in beginning to build a portfolio, they were unlikely to appreciate its potential advantages.

A workshop on portfolio development

On Wednesday morning there was a demonstration of portfolio development. One of the participants volunteered to work with the tutor, observed by the rest of the group, in selecting one item from his or her index and working through the structured questions as outlined in the previous chapter. This proved to be a breakthrough for almost everyone. After this people worked enthusiastically with each other on their portfolios.

Work in pairs/threes

In helping each other to build portfolios, these managers were also developing their coaching and mentoring skills. This was enhanced by the opportunity, within a group of three, for one of the group to observe and, where needed, to facilitate the process. Participants were asked to select an item from their index of experiences which could include any past experience or a current one gained during the training course and that they had already noted in their diaries. They were given the pro-forma illustrated in Figure 3.1 to help with the process.

PORTFOLIO   NAME:

Number (refer to index of experiences):

Description of experience:

⬤

What I learnt from this:

How I can demonstrate that I use what I've learnt:
 (refer to the supporting evidence)

⬤

What I still need to improve in this area:

How I'm going to gain the additional competences, and by when:

Date:

Figure 3.1 *Example of a pro-forma for portfolio development*

Initial presentations of portfolios and action

Towards the end of the week's programme, each person presented something from his or her own portfolio to the rest of the group and to a senior manager who attended this session. In some cases, participants drew on past personal experiences, in some cases on past work or training experiences, and in some cases on experiences that they had gained during the course programme itself. In every case, this was applied to current work practice and in every case there was a commitment given to further learning and to action in the workplace.

The presence of the senior manager gave impetus to the group and a statement of intention to provide support to people in the development of their portfolios and hence their competences.

The competences required

The final part of the week was a review of the work done and of the competences required from the MCI statements. Some of the performance indicators were examined as a way of helping people to consider how they would be able to demonstrate the range of competences required. By now, most people felt sufficiently confident to be able to continue with their portfolio development, with help. They were also able to identify the key areas in which they needed to develop new skills or enhance those that they felt were insufficiently strong.

The following statements made by people at the end of the week give an indication of the kind of commitments being made.

'I thought I knew nothing about finance, so I have been very hesitant in the past about making recommendations for expenditure when my boss has asked me. But having recalled how I've managed my own personal finances and being involved in our social club committee, I realize that I know more than I thought. However, I need to know how to get the information and to involve some of my own staff in thinking through recommendations. I need to get some practice and some help in putting together a proposal for expenditure. I'll discuss this with my boss in the first instance.'

'On this course I have gained some good experience of interviewing somebody. I have the video to put into my portfolio. I want to use this experience as soon as possible at work and I will get involved more in selection interviews as a member of the panel. I also want to make sure that I understand our equal opportunities policy and the legal requirements more fully before I get involved. I will read up on that.'

'What I really want to do is to develop my team. I can use some of the techniques we tried out here. I will look at my self-analysis work and the team-building exercises that we did and put them into my portfolio; but I know that this will only count when I show that I can use it at work.'

'I hadn't realized that part of my role was to get the trust and support of my manager. I thought it was the other way round! I see now it's a two-way thing. I should be keeping her much more informed about what I am doing and generally improving my communication with her. I have already started in a way by developing an action plan which I will be discussing with her when I get back. It's important to improve our working relationship with some of the changes coming up and this is as much my responsibility as my manager's. I will ask for her support.'

'I have discovered from my colleagues here this week just how much I try to take over any discussion. I also saw it from the meetings video we did. I hope you saw an improvement from the later group presentation we made. I'll have them both in my portfolio as a 'before and after' and a reminder to me. I now want to improve the way I participate in meetings; just to make my points without going on and to listen to others more. I will talk to my colleagues at work and my boss and ask them to give me feedback as you have here.'

All the points made were in relation to one or other of the occupational standards required of managers at level 1 of the MCI. The professional development of these participants on the programme had moved forward with the start of their portfolios and would continue once they had carried out their actions and could provide the proof of improving practice.

Follow-up

Since professional development, and therefore portfolio development, is a lengthy procedure, a week's programme is insufficient to do more than begin the process. That is why the initial contract called both for preparatory work that would involve the managers of the learners and for follow-up work of various types. The specifics were left until it became clearer what each group would want and what was considered feasible and appropriate. The following is a sample of what happened with at least two of the groups.

Action at work and with a mentor

Having made their commitments and action plans, individuals met with their manager or a separate mentor to put into practice what they had decided. Not all of this went smoothly, nor within the time-scale that they had anticipated, but almost all did manage to undertake something that made a difference to the work they did and enabled them to show tangible evidence of competence. They ran meetings, carried out new projects, gained information to assist in proposing alternative ways of using computer time, made presentations and dealt with hitherto unresolved staff difficulties.

Reviewing this work with a mentor assisted them in adding to their portfolios and in linking their previous and current competences with those required of them. The evidence they were able to show not only helped progress towards their own professional development, it also gave tangible benefits to the business itself.

Review with work group

After a three-month period, one group of people who worked within the same section met together to review their progress. While most people had managed to make considerable progress, others had not. Few felt very confident about the material they were putting into their portfolio, especially since they had been getting varying opinions from their mentors about what should go into them and what they would be used for.

What they felt they needed was a further session with the tutor to assist them in making sense of some of the practical work they had been undertaking and the material they were beginning to put together. The group negotiated this with the senior manager.

Review in training group

This took place a month later. The group had a refresher workshop on portfolio development and on how to present evidence to show that they had gained the required competences. They then worked in pairs with each other, with tutorial support, to continue with their portfolio-building. This gave them the boost they needed.

Most of the assistance that people need after the first explanation and experience that they have in portfolio development is in the form of confidence-building and reinforcement. Without the support of skilled mentors, without the peer support of the group and without the additional tutorial assistance, it is likely that the individuals will falter in their portfolio-building and therefore in their professional development.

Further action at work and with a mentor

An outcome of the tutorial session was that each person agreed to take continuing action and expressed their confidence (this time often more realistically) about carrying out that action. The participants also had a clearer view of what they wanted from their mentors and felt more able to negotiate a contract with them.

In some cases, the outcomes included a recognition of the fact that two or more of the group could co-operate on a particular project and be far more effective in doing so. On more than one occasion the benefits were visible within a short space of time in terms of better customer service. Participants were able to see the clear link between their portfolio-building, their professional development and the benefits to their organization and the customer. For example, one manager, concerned about communication to customers in a major Inter-City station, developed his motivational and organizational skills with the result that, within three weeks, a simple change meant that information was relayed more efficiently. That had been the action plan of the learner, and I had experienced the results myself on my next visits to the station as a regular traveller. Another satisfied customer!

Regular review in work group

Following this, it was agreed by the group that they would meet on a regular basis about every six weeks. One of the members would convene the meeting and one or two others would structure the session. The main aims were to review progress, to provide support, to share ideas and to decide on new areas of work to enhance their individual competences.

Portfolio development and assessment

As individuals and the group progressed, they became ready to get their portfolios into shape. Up to now they had been in a fairly haphazard form, reflecting the participants' wide variety of experiences and their range of competences. They now needed to sort out what they wanted to show in readiness for the assessment procedure that was being put into place. (See Chapter 10 on organizing a portfolio.)

Using the MCI occupational standards, it became a relatively easy, though sometimes lengthy, task to relate their proof to the required competence. The fact that much material may have been discarded before being seen by the assessor did not detract from the sense of achievement that most of these managers gained both from the work they had done and their recognition of their own abilities.

CASE STUDY 2

Developing portfolios within the work setting

Introduction

In this section I will describe some of the work done with a number of Local Government Authorities, concentrating on some extensive work on portfolio development with Nottinghamshire County Council and Sandwell Metropolitan Borough Council. Although each has developed its portfolio approach in slightly different ways according to needs and the circumstances, they have enough common factors to be looked at together. I will concentrate on the work done with the youth work section of the Leisure Services Departments since there were many similarities in this area.

Part-time workers

In Britain, most youth work is undertaken by part-time adults. A rough guide is that there are around 3,000 full-time youth workers, 30,000 part-time paid workers and 300,000 volunteers. Most of the people responsible for organizing and running youth centres are part time and most of those are, or are expected to be, qualified.

In this case study, the requirement was to improve the way that adults gained their qualification to undertake part-time youth work.

Changing the training approach

The traditional approach to training within the youth service had been much along the lines of training for any other vocation: a basic training course over a number of evenings and weekends concentrating on the skills needed, plus other specialist courses (eg on counselling, canoeing, anti-racist work etc). The desire to change had been the result of two reports, *Starting From Strengths* and *Show What You Know*, the first commissioned by The National Youth Agency, the second by a consortium of national voluntary youth organizations (see Bolger and Scott, 1984, and Redman and Rogers, 1988, in the references).

Recognizing qualities

There were two equally important factors that the organization wanted to take into account when looking at changing its approach. The first was the belief that adults working with young people in youth centres or similar projects, while unqualified, came with a range of abilities that were not recognized. A main aim, therefore, was to discover those abilities and to give people credit for them.

Setting standards

The second factor was that there had been no criteria for establishing quality standards for youth workers. The only qualifying route was through training courses which almost invariably meant that attendance itself was regarded as adequate. There was a desire, therefore, to establish quality standards. In the absence of any national standards at that time, a key task was to establish them locally. This was seen as a positive part of the process, since it was agreed that staff from the organization together with a training manager should work out the standards needed.

Competence statements

One of the objectives was to lay out, as simply as possible, the qualities required of part-time youth workers and the criteria by which they would be assessed. One organization agreed on just four *key roles*, then divided them into *units*, *elements* and *evidence*.

The four key roles were:

- working with young people;
- the curriculum (programme);
- working with other adults; and
- organization and administration.

Below is an excerpt from the competence statements and evidence sought.

KEY ROLES	UNITS	ELEMENTS	EVIDENCE
WORKING WITH YOUNG PEOPLE	1 Empowerment	(i) Making contact with young people individually and in groups.	(a) Recordings of contact made with young people individually and in groups, to include descriptions of the circumstances of the contact.
			(b) Draw a diagram to describe where in the youth centre contact was made with young people.
			(c) Possible use of tape recordings or video to substantiate contacts.
			(d) Observations from supervisor.
		(ii) Establishing trust and openness with young people.	(a) Case study over two to three months to include information on contact established, how relationship developed from initial contact to final discussion with young people.
			(b) Supportive evidence from supervisor.

Figure 3.2 *Excerpt from competence statements for youth workers*

Continuing recruitment

Another factor that was considered as relevant was the relatively small number of people coming forward to take up youth work posts at any one time and that this would be spread throughout the year. This meant that in the past people may have had to wait for up to a year to get the basic training. A more flexible approach was sought that would mean that workers could at least start the process of accreditation within three months of being taken on.

New roles for full-time workers as managers and mentors

One of the implications of changing to a portfolio approach was that people's roles would change. In one organization, instead of running one youth centre each, the full-time staff were given groups of youth clubs and centres to manage within a local patch and asked to oversee the work of key part-time staff. They and others would also take on the responsibility of acting as mentors to any of the unqualified part-time youth workers within their patch to ensure that they received the appropriate support in becoming accredited workers through building up their portfolios.

The consequence of this was that everyone within the organization was asked to take on a higher level of activity. New job descriptions were drawn up in consultation with the staff. There were implications for rates of pay but the overall budget remained at a similar level because fewer staff were needed overall in the changed structure. This was managed without any redundancies. The outcome was a significant increase in levels of morale and motivation among the staff, who had previously become stale and felt undervalued and underused.

Training the mentors

A training programme was carried out for prospective mentors. Most of this was practical; participants had to develop their own portfolios. There were also sessions to explain the process of portfolio development and its purpose within the youth service. Practice on mentoring with tutorial support, together with practical work in the field and feedback on this, made up the final part of the training programme. Mentors were assessed on the basis of their portfolios before being invited to begin taking on that role.

Briefing staff on the portfolio process

The full-time workers, in their role as managers of the process, briefed staff on the new system. The ensuing discussions provided a good opportunity for people to become involved in the changes taking place. Seldom had people at this level been engaged in talking about the training programmes that were offered. Now they showed their knowledge and interest in the questions they asked and from the information they brought to the discussion. The part-timers included people who were also teachers, social workers, shop-owners, factory workers, salespeople, members of the police force and those who were parents, local councillors and students. These were the people who would be providing the supervisory support to the unqualified workers, so it was vital that they were and felt involved in the process from the start.

The portfolio folders

A budget was set aside to ensure that each person going through the accreditation process would be given a ring-binder which would serve as the container for the individual portfolio. Included within the ring-binder was material to give information on the background to the new approach being adopted, the names of the people who would be assisting the learner (the mentor, the supervisor, the assessors), and the statements of competence required together with the kinds of evidence that would be acceptable.

It was emphasized that the contents of the portfolio would remain the property of the learner, who would take the decision as to which parts to submit as evidence of attained competences. The binders were flexible enough to contain photographs or certificates. Learners were encouraged to add other kinds of evidence as supporting material if they wished – for example, tapes, videos, reports or other tangible proof of their abilities.

Induction

Before receiving any of this material, new or recently appointed members of staff went through an induction process with their supervisor, backed up by the mentor. This not only included the usual induction to the work but also to the procedure for accreditation and the portfolio process.

People were asked to develop their index of past experiences and to build up new ones as they became involved in youth work. In this way, by the time they came to develop their stories, these new staff were feeling confident that they had something to offer and were recognizing how they could use some of their experience.

Learning sets

This confidence gave new staff a solid start when coming together with each other and a facilitator. Within three months of starting, a new staff member was invited to join a learning set with seven or eight others who were also seeking accreditation. This was seen as a crucial part of the whole process. The development of portfolios can be, and is often constructed as, a solitary task. While it is true that each individual must be responsible for the construction of his or her own portfolio, there are very good reasons for people working together in groups that provide both support and challenge. This will be dealt with in depth in the next chapter.

The learning set, with the help of a facilitator, was there to share experience and to assist individuals in building their portfolios and identifying common areas where training or additional experience was needed. The learning set met four or five times during the course of a year, according to the group's own needs. In addition, people would meet in pairs or threes at different times to assist each other, take part in joint activities as part of their development and compare notes. The advantages of working in groups as well as alone are significant in terms of the resources saved by the organization and the benefits for individuals.

Mentors

A mentor is, according to *Webster's Dictionary*, 'a trusted counsellor and guide' or, according to the *Penguin English Dictionary*, 'a wise and reliable adviser'. Whichever definition is preferred, the role is a demanding and delicate one, requiring considerable skill and understanding. The term adviser, or personal training adviser, or even tutor, is also used.

In this case study, mentors were drawn from the full-time staff, from experienced and qualified part-time workers and from other professionals outside the organization. They all went through the training programme as described above and once they had developed and submitted their own portfolios they were allocated two or three learners to work with.

Their key tasks were as follows:

- to make themselves available to the learners on an individual basis at a mutually convenient and agreed time, no less than once a month and not more than once a week;
- to outline the process and procedure for portfolio development and for accreditation;

- to *listen* to the learner;
- to provide a framework, as needed, for the learner to develop his or her portfolio (for this, the framework as described in the previous chapter and in Figure 3.1 was used);
- to encourage the learner to consider and record tangible evidence of competence;
- to assist the learner in making a connection between what he or she can do and the competences required to undertake the work;
- to challenge the learner in taking on new activities or learning experiences in order to add to the portfolio those competences that still need to be developed; and
- to offer, where needed, guidance and information on where or how to take on new experiences and on when and how to submit a portfolio for accreditation.

The role of the mentor is to enable and empower the learner to develop his or her own portfolio. The main skills for this are to listen and to ask appropriate and relevant questions. This is where the framework and the pro-forma in Figure 3.1 came in useful for the mentors in the case study. Advice and information is provided where this is factual and based on helping the learner to understand the portfolio process and the resources available for gaining new practice or training. The mentor's role, however, does not include telling the learner what to include in the portfolio or how to record things.

Some of the mentors in the organization portrayed in the case study found this difficult. In particular, some fell into the trap of advising their learners about what to say to their supervisors or how to record a recent experience. Some were used to managing in a more directive way and found it difficult to listen to learners working through an issue quite slowly when they could see a quicker route. Most of those faults were picked up in the training programme for mentors or in later supervision for them.

One of the other problems facing the mentors was the tendency of some to be drawn into a counselling role. Counselling is a considerable skill; in fact the skills of counselling would be useful to anyone acting as a mentor. But there is no place for the mentor to start counselling people as a way of helping them to deal with or resolve personal difficulties. Mentors were advised beforehand to be clear about the boundaries of the discussions they would be having with learners. This was specified by the mentors in the very first session so as to make sure the purpose of the mentoring interviews was clear. Subsequently, when personal issues arose on two or three occasions that were difficult for the learner, the mentor gently but firmly reminded the person that he or she was not in a position to offer personal counselling.

Some learners may, for one reason or another, find it difficult to write down or otherwise record their experiences and competences, often because it is an unfamiliar process for them. They need longer to get into the process and need more patience and encouragement than most. Others may have a physical disability. Someone who is dyslexic may be most uncomfortable about putting something on paper. Several of our mentors encountered this situation. They encouraged the learners to use a tape recorder or on occasions wrote things down as the learner dictated. The important thing was the relationship of trust built up between mentor and learner.

One mentor worked with a man who was almost totally physically disabled through multiple sclerosis. The learner worked with other groups of physically disabled young people, teaching them to use a computer. Using his own computer, pressing each key with a lever attached to his head, he conversed with his mentor and completed his portfolio. The mentor needed to learn a great deal about patience and the significance of being disabled.

Since most people who will act as mentors or advisers will be doing this for the first time as part of another role, and may even be the manager of the portfolio-builder, it is worth while recognizing that the role is probably *the* key one in the assistance given to portfolio developers.

A very useful section on mentors, or advisers, is given in Susan Simosko's book, *APL: A Practical Guide for Professionals*, published by Kogan Page.

Supervisors

The supervisors in the case study were normally the line managers of the new staff who were going through the portfolio process.

Supervisors were briefed about the process and their role. They appreciated the approach, partly because it gave them a clearer role in relation to their newer staff and partly because it encouraged the new staff to take on different activities in their youth work, rather than just going away on training courses to learn. One problem for some supervisors was that it challenged them to the point of threatening their normal ways of doing things. Since that outcome was part of the effort to raise quality throughout the youth service, it was seen by the organizers as being a positive factor, although it had to be dealt with delicately.

The supervisors' role was:

- to ensure that the induction of new workers took place, including the explanation of the portfolio and accreditation process and the roles of mentors and the others involved;
- to meet regularly with the learner, not less than once every two weeks in the work setting;
- to provide new work opportunities as requested by the learner, either within the work setting or in conjunction with other sections or centres;
- to give feedback to the learner on the work he or she has undertaken;
- to provide substantiating evidence of the learner's competence on specific tasks for his or her portfolio; and
- to agree with the learner the time to be taken for additional training.

Facilitators

Since learning sets were an integral part of the process, facilitators were engaged to assist small groups of learners to work with each other as a self-managed learning group. This meant, as with the mentors, that the facilitator was not there to teach but to enable and empower.

Experienced group workers were brought in to undertake this work since it is a demanding role (though it may appear easy). Fortunately youth work has a rich source of people who can work successfully with groups in this way. In other settings this may not be the case. Good team leaders, or people who can chair meetings well without imposing their own ideas and judgements, may have the kind of qualities required.

The development of good facilitators for the portfolio process is another positive reason for encouraging it within organizations, for the good facilitator is likely to be able to delegate well, to motivate teams, to empower others to take on more responsibility and to encourage development generally within groups of staff. He or she may not necessarily have the qualities of inspiring or leading others from the front, but can almost certainly help others to reach their own inspiration and to take the lead for themselves. In the future, that may become a key role within organizations.

The facilitator's role in the case study was:

- to convene the learning set;
- to explain its purpose and the respective roles of the facilitator and the group;
- to invite members of the group to discuss their progress and their difficulties in working on their portfolios;
- to review the common issues that had been raised within the group;
- to encourage the members of the learning set to practise portfolio development with each other;
- to arrive at agreements on the joint learning requirements and the action or training needed; and
- to liaise with mentors and trainers on the learning requirements and training programme offered.

Training

Rather than offer a predetermined training programme, training was tailor-made to the needs of the learners. There were some clear advantages to this as well as some difficulties to be overcome.

The advantages were:

- people only received training in what they needed, and in the way they needed it;
- the learners felt responsible for their own learning and therefore 'owned' it;
- learners were open to the training and actively involved in the programmes; and

- learners were far more questioning than on previous programmes and able to take on ideas and concepts with greater
alacrity.

The difficulties were:

- in responding to training requests, trainers had to be quicker
and more flexible in providing a relevant programme and
finding the appropriate tutors;
- tutors were not always familiar with the portfolio process
and needed reminding to include a portion of time within
each session for learners to add to their portfolios; and
- numbers of learners, the times that they wanted specific
training and the availability of resources meant that it was
sometimes hard to put together a package when wanted.

Most of the difficulties were turned to good use as learners became
more adept at managing their own learning and discovering their
own ways of getting the training they wanted. One learning set
negotiated with the trainer and got an outside tutor to run a series
of workshops on equal opportunities. Another group of three went
on a course to learn instructor skills for outdoor activities. One
person engineered a free place on a management course at a local
management college. Six others enrolled on a first aid course run
by the Red Cross.

Portfolio contents

During the course of the whole programme, learners had been
developing their portfolios, based on the five main steps described
earlier. The time they took to build their portfolios to the stage of
wanting to submit them for accreditation varied. The shortest
amount of time was just under six months. This person had previously undertaken youth work for some years in another organization but had no qualifications. She had been able to use a great
deal of her previous experience and provide evidence for her portfolio that demonstrated her competences without her needing further training at this level. The average amount of time was around
12 months, with some taking up to 18 months or more to submit
their portfolios.

Portfolios included:

- an **index** of experiences, cross-referenced to indicate the competences demonstrated;
- summaries of the **stories** of each experience;
- summaries of the **discoveries** gained from each experience;
- **proof** of current competence – eg reports, certificates, letters, minutes, photos, taped interviews, project work, programme plans, newspaper cuttings, references;
- summaries of learning needs identifying the personal **ownership** of the learner for those needs and for taking action on them;
- summaries and evidence of the **growth** points indicating the plans of the learner for gaining new competences; and
- a **review** of the learning processes and results, showing evidence of new competences gained by the learner and a final summary showing how and where in the portfolio the required competences were all demonstrated.

Assessment

In this case, the required competence statements had been developed by the local government authority itself, using a similar format to that employed within the NVQ standards. The panel who had developed the statements was drawn from professionals and volunteers in the field of youth work, some from within the organization and some from outside, acting as consultants.

The assessment procedure was that a panel was appointed for this purpose, also consisting of a mix of professionals, experienced volunteer workers and an external adviser. The trainer for the organization was the convener and arbiter. In the event of any complaint or dissent, an appeals procedure was put into effect.

The time for submitting a portfolio was left very much in the hands of the learner, in consultation with his or her mentor and supervisor. The role of the assessment panel was:

- to be familiar with the required competences at the appropriate level being assessed and with the portfolio process;
- to look at the portfolios submitted (in practice, individual panel members took responsibility for going through a

specific portfolio, making notes on it and making recommendations to the rest of the panel);

- to review the *breadth* of experience shown by the portfolio (is it enough?);
- to review the *depth* of experience shown by the portfolio (does it go far enough?);
- to consider the *relevance* of the experience and how this is shown (does it demonstrate competences that we are seeking?);
- to examine the *validity* of the evidence shown (does it demonstrate that the learner can really do this?);
- to consider the *development* shown by the learner's readiness to include the take-up of new learning opportunities;
- to assess whether the person has satisfactorily demonstrated the required competences (there was no question of somebody 'failing' – either they had or had not yet demonstrated all the competences in their portfolio);
- to decide upon one of three options:
  - (a) to recommend accreditation
  - (b) to indicate to the learner what had not been satisfactorily completed and to ask for those competences not yet shown to be submitted at a later date
  - (c) to invite the learner to meet with the panel and respond to questions for clarification.

Chapter 4

Portfolios for Team Development

One of the discoveries I made in the course of working with people on their portfolios was that the process had an effect on others as well. Inevitably, work colleagues, friends and family members were influenced by the personal discoveries an individual was making during the course of building a portfolio. Most significantly, this was seen when a team worked together to assist each other in portfolio development. The result is that not only do individuals develop, but so does the team if we learn how to use the process in a team setting.

This chapter will focus on the experience of building individual portfolios for team development, rather than on the development of team portfolios – although the latter may often be a useful and positive spin-off.

In describing the process and practical purposes of portfolio-building within teams, I will draw on the experience of working mainly with an area management team from a hairdressing company, whom I will call Hair Carers, and a team of managers of local Citizens' Advice Bureaux (CABs) in the North West of England. The National Association of CABs is a charity providing a network of information and advice centres based in almost every town and city in Britain and open to anyone who needs advice on benefits or assistance available to them.

Objectives

My work with these organizations was as an external consultant. The processes to be used are similar whether you are working as a manager or as an internal trainer or consultant. There are many ways in which it is easier as an outside consultant to clarify the objective that an organization may have in wanting to develop its teams. The consultant can ask apparently basic but crucial questions to establish why a client wants something; whereas, working from the inside, the trainer or manager may make assumptions about what is wanted. Assumptions cause misunderstandings and breakdowns in communication. It is always important to ask why we are doing something before going too far down the road of doing it because it seems a good idea.

The objectives given by the clients in this case for asking me to work with their teams included the following:

- to enhance the targeted performance of individual team members;
- to improve particular skills – for example, appraisal, coaching, project management;
- to develop teamwork in order to encourage a more cohesive approach to the work and raise the quality of delivery; and
- to encourage support from within the team so as to reduce a sense of isolation and heighten confidence and morale.

Those objectives arose out of the initial request to 'do some team development work'. It was necessary to clarify the requirements in order to focus the work and be able to monitor the programme effectively. It would be the results at work, not just the report of the participants, however favourable, that would determine the effectiveness of what we had done.

Contract with the client

In exploring the possibility of and the potential for using portfolios as a means of achieving the objectives, it is necessary to be clear about the implications for others in the organization. Agreements need to be reached beforehand about such things as the kind and level of support that will be needed, how information from the team is to be communicated to others, and what is to be monitored and how.

The points that were agreed with Hair Carers included:

- reports would be given on a regular basis to the manager of the programme, to include the main general issues that had been raised, the specific skills that had been addressed, the projects and action plans that had been agreed by team members and any requests for change or action made by the team to the manager;
- specific individual issues would remain confidential to the team and would not be included in any report;
- portfolios would be presented to the manager by the individual concerned as part of an appraisal system, and the appraisal system itself would take into account the portfolio process;
- the manager would ensure that any requests for action or change were looked at in depth and, where feasible and appropriate, dealt with; and
- after evaluation of the programme, where appropriate, a strategy would be developed to extend the use of portfolios for team development across the organization.

The area CAB wanted the following points in its contract:

- individual bureau managers to gain support from each other and improve how they support others not in this group;
- the focus to be on personal development, with each person clarifying his or her own needs and working on them;
- to practise processes to deal with problems at work;
- to consider how to disseminate this work and how to relate it to other CABs; and
- an evaluation to be made at regular intervals of the practical benefits gained.

Such a contract is not easy to achieve at the beginning of what will be to most a new programme using unfamiliar methods with unknown consequences. It is only with the benefit of hindsight that I can say that this is the ideal. In neither of the two organizations I am describing did we arrive at a comprehensively satisfactory agreement beforehand. In one case, the contract emerged over a lengthy period while the programme was going on. The result was that the whole process took much longer to become absorbed into the organization than it otherwise might have done.

Contract with the team

Since one of the aspects of portfolio development is to encourage a sense of ownership of one's own abilities and actions, it is as vital to establish a contract with the members of each new team as it is with an individual or the organization's representative. It is also a more delicate operation. There are two main common difficulties.

The first is that some team members may not agree with what the majority is putting forward, but will not be prepared to speak out for fear of being seen as different or difficult. This can be a problem even where the team is a long-established one, since the beginning of a new process like this will invariably make it less comfortable for individuals to stand out. In one team, for example, the issue of reporting back progress to the senior manager came up. Most of the team agreed that this was appropriate, but one person felt that everything should be kept confidential within the group, otherwise it could inhibit the discussion and undermine the value of ownership that he believed we were trying to engender. In this case, the person did raise his dissension from the start, with the result that the issue was clarified and eventually agreed by everyone with greater understanding. Had he not pointed out his concern, reporting back could have had a very different meaning to some members of the group and at least one person would have remained very uncomfortable with the contract.

The second difficulty is that as the process establishes itself, some agreements made in the initial contract may need to be changed. Sometimes members are faced with having broken the contract and dealing with the implications of that. On one occasion, a team was confronted with the fact that three of its eight members had not carried out their agreed action from the previous time. As a result, an agreement was added to the contract that pairs of team members would telephone each other to check on progress and to provide support where this was needed. The result was that,

by the time people came to each team session, they were always
well prepared, having undertaken some piece of work that had
been recorded for portfolio development and presentation to the
rest of the team.

Extracts of a team contract that was agreed are as follows:

- team members will make every effort to attend these meetings;
- the purpose of the sessions is to enhance individual performance, to improve defined skills, to develop team work and
  to provide support;
- individual issues discussed within the team will remain confidential to the group;
- members will carry out any agreed action and will report on
  the results of that action to the rest of the team;
- each member will keep a record of his or her achievements
  for a portfolio to be shared with other members of the team;
- members will listen to each other and respect each other's
  views; and
- we will challenge and accept challenges positively.

The inclusion of a portfolio element into the contract came once
I had introduced the concept and given practical evidence to the
team that this was a productive process. This meant that this part
of the contract tended to come after the others. In some cases, the
stage of the team is such that it may take quite a long time before
it is appropriate to introduce the idea of portfolio-building. The
team facilitator must make an assessment of this. One of the essential ingredients is that the team has to have the skills and the
attitudes needed to provide each other with support and challenge.
This means that some preparatory work must take place before
inviting the team to develop portfolios.

Skills development

Probably the most valuable outcome of portfolio development is
that people gain some positive and useful skills during the process
itself. Done individually, people develop skills in analysing and
recording, in reflecting and making connections, in managing

personal learning, and in presenting themselves. They also gain in confidence and in the ability to make clearer decisions about themselves and their work.

Portfolio development in groups enhances other skills too. Listening actively and constructively, a much underused skill, is improved. Learning to recognize, acknowledge and balance the strengths and weaknesses of team members is another gain, as is the ability to confront and deal positively with problems. In terms of attitudes, an understanding and an acceptance of each others' differences has been a common change within teams. There has also often been an increased desire to share ideas and practical work with other members of the team, to the obvious benefit of the whole organization.

Sometimes teams already have most of those skills; at other times they will be lacking. The team facilitator will need to gain an understanding of the level of those skills and the attitudes within the team. This can be done most productively in discussion with the team itself. It is worth while making some assessment and, where needed, working with the team on developing some of the skills needed before starting on portfolio-building. Some training sessions on problem solving, on active-listening processes, on peer support and on questioning techniques may be helpful to the team in preparation for portfolio work.

A process for team development using portfolios

Just as there is a process for individual personal and professional development, there is a process for team development. Later on I will illustrate how the two processes relate to each other and how they both relate to organizational development.

The five main aspects of individual portfolio development are matched by five for team development (as shown in Figure 4.1). They are:

1. strengths: 'what we have';
2. the competences required of us: 'what we need';
3. action and training: 'what we did and what we learnt';
4. team review: 'how we've done'; and

5. appraisal: 'what have we gained and what's next?'

1. Strengths: 'what we have'

The whole point about using portfolios as a development process is that it enables us to start with our strengths instead of the usual assumption that if it's training or development it must begin with our weaknesses. In working with teams the starting point is therefore to establish the strengths of the team. Two effective ways to do this are:

1. to work together with the team in compiling a list of its joint attributes; or
2. to invite individuals to develop their own portfolios first and then to pool the main strengths of everyone.

The first option is probably the ideal, but I am reminded of the first time I invited a team to say what its strengths were. Everyone told me about his or her weaknesses and what was wrong with the team. I reverted to option two, using the framework for individual development, and asked people to talk in pairs about some of their experiences. From this, each person then shared one key experience and what had been gained from it. The ensuing list and discussion was remarkable. For the first time, it appeared, members of the team recognized abilities in themselves and each other that could be of great value if only they were known about.

The area managers from Hair Carers gave as some of the strengths within the team:

> practical experience of hairdressing
> experience of running a business
> quality award for training
> lots of energy and enthusiasm
> ability to deal with people at all levels
> can work under pressure.

Not everyone claimed to have all these strengths, but everyone contributed to the list and recognized that between them they could offer a considerable amount to the company. After compiling the list, each person was asked to say what experience those strengths were based on and how they could demonstrate them.

This work constituted the first session. As part of their action between then and the next session a month later, team members were asked to record their individual and then their team strengths for their portfolio.

Up to then, this team had felt undervalued and overworked and this had affected their own sense of self-esteem both individually and as a group. Most of their previous meetings had consisted of briefings from their manager, looking at statistical information, reacting to staff changes in the salons, and dealing with supplies of equipment or other problems facing branches. In sharing their strengths with each other, they remarked how much more positive they felt about themselves and began to see themselves as a team for the first time.

Part of the contract with the team, accepted by the company, was that the senior manager was not present during these team sessions. Whether the advantages of this outweigh the disadvantages will depend on the circumstances. In this case, and where the prime consideration was team development, it would not have been appropriate or helpful for the manager to have been there during the early stages. Later on, however, as the team developed and became more confident, a new contract was negotiated so that the manager did attend and become involved with at least part of the process. When she experienced the process and heard the strengths within the team, she changed the style of her own meetings with them and encouraged far more participation and sharing of ideas.

2. The competences required of us: 'what we need'

The second aspect, and the second step of portfolio-building for team development, is for the team to explore and decide what competences they actually need to carry out their work effectively to a high standard.

Where national standards are defined there is a valuable yardstick by which any group can decide upon its own specific needs. If individuals within a team are going forward to acquire vocational or professional accreditation through this method, then they will in any case need to demonstrate all the competences within their own level. In looking at portfolios for team development we need to ensure that, whether or not there are nationally stated standards of competence, the team itself spends some time on exploring what those standards are and how they relate to the specific work. This again is the issue of ownership. The team that has defined its own standards is more likely to take responsibility for ensuring that everyone attains those standards.

The competences defined by the CAB managers included the following:

> to manage paid and voluntary staff
> to pass on knowledge of advice and information systems
> to ensure the maintenance of adequate records
> to prepare budgets and maintain budgetary controls
> to assist management committees in planning policies
> to ascertain local needs and implement strategies to meet those needs

Within each of those units of competence, the team considered the elements and the performance criteria. For example, under 'to manage paid and voluntary staff', the elements were seen as:

> assessment of staff needs
> recruitment of paid and voluntary staff ensuring compliance with equal opportunities
> carrying out interviews
> providing an induction programme for new staff
> ensuring that all staff receive training as appropriate
> running staff meetings
> etc, etc

Performance criteria for 'running staff meetings', for example, were agreed as:

> meeting with staff on a regular basis (not less than monthly)
> giving advance notice of meetings
> preparing a detailed agenda and advising staff beforehand
> planning the meeting to ensure that items are dealt with properly
> chairing the meeting to ensure:
> – full participation by staff in discussion
> – control is kept

- a summary of the main discussion points is made
- decisions are made as needed
- proper records are kept, with action points noted

ensuring that action points are followed up and carried out as agreed

giving opportunities to meet with individual staff as requested

Through the process of defining their own competence statements as a team, there were two main consequences.

The first was that the CAB team became much more rigorous in seeing what had to be done and the competences they needed to have in relation to the strengths they had identified. This meant that they went back to those strengths and redefined some of them more sharply.

The second was that they recognized, individually and corporately, where they did not have the required competences to the standard they themselves thought necessary. As a corollary to that, they saw that some of the team could provide adequate evidence to show that they were good at the things others felt weak on.

3. Action and training: 'what we did and what we learnt'

The connection between 'what we have' and 'what we need' leads directly to the team being able to decide what it needs to learn and plan to take up relevant learning opportunities. There may well be individual needs that differ from what the rest of the team wants. These can be dealt with by those people negotiating their own learning contract either with the rest of the team or separately with a mentor.

In the case of both the CAB's and Hair Carers' area managers, the teams developed and managed their own training programme. They also helped each other to plan the relevant action in the workplace to enable individuals to develop the required competence. For team development, this is the essence of portfolio-building. Each person has a hand in their own and each other's development. An example will illustrate this: In the Hair Carers area managers' team, one of the elements of competence required was 'to recruit and select salon managers'. Staff turnover had been high for the previous year during a time of expansion, so area managers had spent a considerable amount of time in finding and appointing new managers, a number of whom had not turned out to be suitable. This had been costly to the company and damaging to its service and reputation.

One of the performance criteria that had been defined was 'to carry out selection interviews that determine the suitability of candidates for the job'. The team decided that, from their record and their own lack of previous training in this area, they needed to develop their skills in selection interviewing.

A one-day workshop on selection interviewing took place, concentrating specifically on raising skills in preparation and questioning techniques that established how candidates had behaved in previous situations similar to those expected of them. Since three of the six team members had interviews planned over the subsequent three weeks, the team agreed to work in pairs to prepare and run these interviews. In this way each person got some practice and each pair was able to give and receive feedback. In the following team development session, individuals shared their portfolio recording with the rest of the team. The outcomes were:

- each team member had some tangible evidence recorded in his or her portfolio of enhanced competence in interviewing;
- the team was able to demonstrate how it had improved its performance in this respect; and
- the three salon managers who had been selected all proved to be good appointees and further interviews over the next six months proved similarly successful.

The CAB team had identified as one difficulty the problems most managers had in working with their own management committees on defining clear policies, particularly at a time of decreased funding and increased demand on services. Two of the eight felt that they had managed to deal with this to their satisfaction. These two discussed their experience and how they had overcome difficulties. As a result, the other six identified specific problems and how they would tackle them. One manager saw her problem as having an uncommitted management committee who delayed taking crucial decisions. The immediate issue was that an opportunity for new and much improved offices had emerged. There were financial implications, but grants were available for such a project from a regional fund, as long as applications were made. The services offered by the CAB were severely hampered by its current premises.

After discussing this at the team development session, the manager decided upon the following action:

- to make an appointment to see the chairman;
- to present the chairman with a brief, outlining the opportunities for the CAB in making the move, the funding available and the willingness of staff to take this on;
- to ask the chairman what he thought was holding the committee back from taking a decision; and
- to propose that a special development group be established to oversee the arrangements.

The manager went away and implemented her plan of action.

Her portfolio in the subsequent 12 months included:

- a summary of the problems and how this was limiting services offered to clients;
- her action plan;
- recordings of the discussion held with her chairman;
- a summary of the difficulties being faced by the management committee;
- relevant minutes of meetings with an agreed development strategy;
- a copy of the application for funding;
- invitations sent to a prospective development group;
- notes of development group meetings;
- letters negotiating the purchase of the new offices;
- plans outlining how new offices space would be used;
- a plan of new services that could be established;
- a letter from funders showing grant approved;
- confirmation of new offices purchased;
- Annual General Meeting notes, with congratulations from chairman and showing make-up of new management committee which included members of the development group;
- a report from her manager reviewing start of new services and improvement of old; and

- photographs of the old and new offices.

Throughout the 12 months that this person's portfolio showed how her competence and confidence developed, she was supported by the other team members in the monthly sessions. She did not always take the opportunity to discuss progress on this project in much depth, but the issues presented and discussed by other members helped her to reflect on her own circumstance. In addition, the informal contact that developed between these eight people was such that regular phone conversations or informal meetings meant that she was frequently able to say what action she was taking and what the results had been.

4. Team review: 'how we've done'

The individual work and the joint training undertaken by members of the team is entered into each person's portfolio. In normal team development work it is often the case that people fail to see what has actually happened to change things, or even that there have been any changes. The portfolio process means that a continuing record is kept of changes as they take place, of lessons learnt and of further work to be done.

Even keeping an individual portfolio may not mean that the team as a whole is conscious of its own growth unless the collection of portfolios is reviewed from time to time. Part of the process of portfolio-building is to be able to see development. The effect this has on self-confidence, self-esteem, personal motivation and overall standards is immeasurable for individuals. In teams, the sense of joint achievement, status and power can be added to those other qualities. There are implications for the rest of the organization in this. The CAB team, for example, became seen as the most articulate, able and powerful group of managers within their region. The Youth Service team in Sandwell, the subject matter for one of the case studies in the last chapter, was seen in a similar light by their managers and colleagues in other departments.

This can have positive or negative results. In the CAB region, the team was seen as something of a threat to other managers and as a clique seeking only power and status. This diminished after the team became aware of their image and sought to change it, and also as a result of other managers forming their own team development groups. In Sandwell, the results were positive. The team was seen as an example of good practice and training policy was modelled on their experience.

The Hair Carers team was the full complement of area managers within the company. The effects on others were both positive and negative. The negative consequence was that the senior manager felt challenged by the team to the extent that she began to block some of the proposals for action that they were making. Her involvement in the later sessions of the team development meetings, and the undeniable proof of real and beneficial changes, enabled her to turn her negativity into a positive benefit. She began to delegate more to the area team, leaving herself more time to concentrate on longer term strategy. Her confidence in the team increased and relationships became more positive and productive as a result. The longer term consequence of the portfolio-building team development process was in the company's increased profitability, achieved primarily through the key managerial team becoming more competent and confident.

The review procedure itself is held between six and twelve months after the start of the team process. This is a review not of the individual successes, but of the progress of the team itself. There are two key questions for the team to address:

1. what have we achieved as a team?
2. how have we got there?

These questions will relate to the objectives and the contract. It is both the *content* of what the team has done and the *process* by which it has worked together. The portfolio approach emphasizes both content and process equally and this is mirrored in any review procedure.

The CAB team saw a whole list of achievements including the following five:

'we are clearer about our management tasks and better about carrying them out';

'we have been able to improve the way meetings are run at regional level with a wider cross-section of managers';

'we have provided much support for each other in helping to enhance individual managers' work';

'we have seen improvements in the quality of service in all our bureaux';

'our morale has improved despite greater demands on our services with less resources'.

Each of those and the other achievements were explored in greater detail, with examples given. Into the portfolio of each went the team review headings, together with the specific instances relating to that individual manager.

The team then looked at how they had worked together to achieve those things. Their summaries included:

'we listened to each other';

'we made sure we supported each other in carrying out agreed action';

'we decided on our training needs';

'we recorded what we did'.

5. Appraisal: 'what have we gained and what's next?'

The appraisal process is almost always seen as an individual procedure between manager and staff member. In the portfolio team development process the need for individual staff appraisal is minimized. In this, as in many other respects, the process is akin to the kind of quality approaches inspired by Edwards Deming and his followers. The full portfolio model will illustrate the place of appraisal in relation to individual and organizational development later on.

The essence here is peer appraisal, sometimes but by no means always involving the manager in the process as well. The team can now reflect back on its overall achievements in the workplace by asking two questions – each of which should be put to the team and to its individual members.

The two questions – 'what have we gained?' and 'what's next?' – are different in context from each other and subtly, but necessarily, different from the review stage. In this case, the emphasis is on

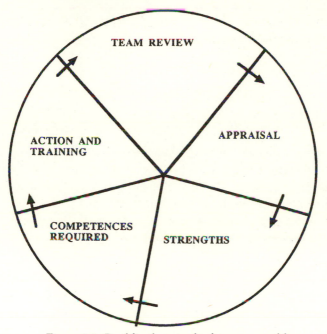

Figure 4.1 *Portfolios for team development: a model*

how individuals and the team have performed during the previous six or at most twelve months in the workplace. This is the time for individual presentations and feedback, and for the team as a whole to agree what its main achievements have been against work objectives. All that provides evidence for individual portfolios. Team members are acting as each other's mentors. In the healthiest of organizations, the manager will be part of that process too, giving and receiving feedback in the role of manager to the rest of the team. The result is that people manage themselves much more effectively.

The second part of this stage is the planning part. There will be organizational, team and individual work objectives. Those, too, can be put into individuals' portfolios even though only some of the team will be personally responsible for achieving them. This means that the team as a whole is constantly aware of each other's goals and that part of their continuing team development work is to monitor the progress of those goals and, where needed, provide support in achieving them.

In answer to the first question, 'what have we gained?', for example, Hair Carers reported:

- greater stability in staff, with a decrease from ten managers lost last year to three this year;
- better communication with salon managers, leading to increased efficiency within salons;
- increase in custom in 75 per cent of our salons by over 15 per cent, with the others maintaining their turnover during a time of general downturn in the trade;
- above target on all our productivity goals this year; and
- decrease in wastage, including savings in purchasing small items, of 10 per cent.

Team facilitation

Most people working with a group will use their own methods. I have already described the stages to be gone through when working with individuals and over the long term with teams. In this section I am going to describe a useful method of group facilitation specifically designed for team development using a portfolio approach. It is a method I have used extensively and successfully across a whole range of groups and organizations. Once demonstrated and practised, its beauty is that it can be picked up and used by any team for their own continuing development. I am indebted to the late Professor Eugene Heimler for introducing the idea behind the method. It is called 'group dialogue'.

Before starting the group dialogue, the facilitator should outline the process and establish a contract with the group on its ground rules. Such ground rules may include:

- confidentiality;
- openness;
- no interruptions;
- everyone participating as requested;
- honesty; and
- issues to do with our work only.

The rules, especially the last, will depend upon the group and its purpose.

About 45 minutes is an average amount of time for one group dialogue session, with a group of between six and eight people being the optimum number to work with.

The objective for the group dialogue is for the team to assist one of its members to work out a plan for dealing with a specific issue that he or she is facing at that time. For the purposes of illustration, I will use extracts from one of the Hair Carers managers' sessions. The same method was used for the CAB team in which the manager resolved to carry out her plan described earlier for dealing with a reluctant management committee and get better office accommodation.

There are seven steps in the group dialogue. They are:

1. **presentation**;
2. **clarification**;
3. **team summaries**;
4. **presenter's summary**;
5. **action ideas**;
6. **presenter's action; and**
7. **review of process and wider implications.**

1. Presentation

The first step is to invite one member of the team to talk about something that he or she needs to resolve or deal with. I sometimes ask the whole team to jot down something of current concern which they have to handle. The issue may be to do with an overload of work, a staff member causing difficulties, a project coming up that needs thinking about, a recurrent complaint from customers, or anything that is causing some concern to the individual team member.

One area manager, whom I shall call Tim, presented the following:

'Having established a good training programme and having linked it to our award system for best trainee hairdresser of the year, I've found that three of my eight branch managers are just not supporting it. They say that they'd rather train their people themselves and not have them keep going off for a day every week, especially when they have a lot of trainees. The problem is they put up a good economic argument, but I'm not happy that standards are as good as they should be. The other thing is that the staff in those salons see themselves as above everyone else, so they don't even regard our awards as being an incentive.'

2. Clarification

After the individual has made his or her uninterrupted presentation, the facilitator asks the rest of the team to ask any questions that would help to clarify what they have heard. The facilitator needs to prevent people from jumping to answers – 'what you need to do...' – personal anecdotes like 'I had the same problem down in...' or redefining the issue: 'what you mean is...'. The aim of the portfolio approach is to empower people to define their own needs and action, and the facilitator's task here is to enable the team to carry out that empowerment. The questions are asked not just to clarify things for the questioner, but to help the presenter become clearer about what he or she is saying. This is probably the longest part of the session and the most crucial. In answering the questions, a more detailed picture will emerge.

Some of the questions asked in this case were:

'What is your relationship with those three managers?'

'What do you think it is about those three branches that makes them feel superior?'

'What have you actually said to them?'

'What do you mean when you say the standards are not as good in their training?'

Those questions and others were answered by the presenter until each of the team was satisfied that they understood what the main factors were.

3. Team summaries

One of the strengths in working with a team in this way is that there will be a variety of equally valid perceptions of what has been said. Because each person may pick up different things or put different emphases on certain aspects, the presenter is left with a richer version.

This step consists of the facilitator asking each member of the team to write down a summary of what he or she has heard the presenter say. They are asked to pick out the key points, rather than to regurgitate the whole of what has been said. People write the summaries in this way for two reasons. First, they will be much more succinct when they are asked to read back their summaries, otherwise they will tend to ramble on. Second, the summaries are raw material for the presenter's portfolio.

Once everyone has written down a summary, he or she reads it out. Here are some samples:

'Tim said that he is having difficulty in persuading three of his branch managers to fall in line with his training programme. He feels intimidated by them and doesn't want to upset them. He is not certain in any case that they are wrong.'

'The problem that Tim has presented lies in his uncertainty with the training and award scheme. He has not been able to make a positive case to put to his managers and is letting their action undermine his confidence in the scheme. He has not asked them for their views on the programme.'

'Tim has got five of his eight managers involved in the training programme. The three others have not taken part and Tim is concerned that their standard of training does not conform in a number of small respects to what is required. Tim sees that the managers have a case, but as yet has not been able to persuade them or himself that his programme is better.'

4. Presenter's summary

The presenter listens to the summaries being read by the other members of the team without commenting, but may want to make notes. The facilitator then asks the presenter to make his or her own summary. It often happens that this summary, that is to say the presenter's understanding of the issue, has changed considerably from the original statements made as a result of getting this feedback.

Tim's summary was:

> 'I realize that I feel intimidated by these three managers, who have all been in the job longer than me. That has stopped me from putting forward strongly the benefits of this training programme for their branches and the whole company. I am clear about it, but I have not got that across. The other thing it has prevented me from doing is asking them how they could support the programme. My main concern is that we have a cohesive programme supported by all so that all trainees get a good experience of our training and take a pride in working for the company, not just their own branch. I haven't put that across at all.'

5. Action ideas

Once the presenter has made his or her own summary the facilitator asks the others to consider what has just been said. What would they do in that position? Each person is asked to write down his or her own plan of action ready to read out to the presenter.

Some of the action ideas read out were:

> 'Write a memo outlining the main advantages of the training and award scheme and ask all the managers to respond to it.'

> 'I'd meet with the three managers individually and put to them why I want the programme to succeed and ask them what their objections really are. If there are strong objections, I would work out a compromise, asking for half of their trainees to come on the scheme for a trial period.'

> 'I think Tim has to develop a much better understanding with these three managers. I would ask for their assistance and ideas as to how to make this work; or for their suggestions as to how to improve it.'

> 'I would run the scheme as it is for a year. If it's good I'd try to get it company policy that everyone takes part; then they would have to be involved.'

6. Presenter's action

The action ideas are seldom going to be exactly the same, and in this case they were very varied. Responsibility for the action, however, lies with the presenter, since it is his or her issue that is being resolved. Having listened to the other action ideas, the presenter usually makes a synthesis of the feasible ones, given the circumstances. The action ideas are all passed on to the presenter for his or her portfolio. The facilitator now asks for the presenter's action. This is what Tim said:

> 'I'm going to meet with each of the three. I'll write down what I want to say first. I will say what the point of the programme is and its benefits. I will also say what my concerns are, about a common training experience of high standards and about their non-involvement and 'separatism'. I'll also say that I need their support for the scheme to be fully successful and that I understand their own staffing problems. Then I will ask for their ideas on how to reach our goals.'

7. Review of process and wider implications

At first glance it may appear that a lot of time is spent on one person; in fact, on just one issue. What invariably happens, however, is that almost everyone in the team relates something of the circumstance and solution to his or her own situation. Apart from that, there is the recognition that the team is able to provide support for each of its members in dealing with difficult and sometimes apparently unresolvable work issues. This final step in the group dialogue provides the team with the opportunity to reflect on two things: how they actually worked together as a group and the wider implications for the team from this issue.

The facilitator first goes through the seven steps of the group dialogue. This will be in preparation for another member of the team to act as facilitator the next time. The facilitator also asks the team, starting with the presenter, to consider how the process worked.

In this case some of the comments were:

'I really felt listened to and it was amazing how I realized what I had or hadn't been doing.'

'It was much easier than I thought being able to summarize what Tim said, because that's all I had to concentrate on.'

'It wasn't like any other kind of meeting. There didn't seem to be any competition and it was very supportive, yet we didn't pull our punches.'

'We kept to the task well. The structure really helped with that. It seemed very forced at first but it would never have worked without it.'

The facilitator then asks the team to think what implications may arise from the issue and action points put forward by the presenter. The comments were:

'Tim should carry out his action and report back on progress to the team.'

'We need to get on better terms with some of our branch managers. Our communication is very patchy and I think we spend too much time with the ones we get on with rather than the ones we have difficulty with.'

'We don't use the experience of some of our really good managers because we probably do feel intimidated by them. In future I'm going to ask for more of their ideas and support and I think we should agree that we all do that and how we're going to do it.'

The team set the following action plan for itself: the team members would record their progress in their portfolios and report back on how they improved communication with their managers and what the outcomes were.

Follow-up

Those are the seven steps in the group dialogue process, but there is a follow-up – since this is about team development and since the portfolio process is a continual one. In this case there were two main areas to follow up on: the results of the presenter's action and

the outcomes of the team's agreed action. The issue, the action and
the outcome is recorded in people's portfolios so that they can be
accurately reported at a later team development meeting.

In this case the outcome reported by Tim and recorded in his
portfolio was:

> 'I carried out my plan. It just worked out that I met first with the
> manager I find the most difficult. I kept to my brief and I kept
> my head. By the end of our meeting I felt he had mellowed
> considerably, although he was still very cautious about getting
> involved and he was adamant about his training being better, or
> at least as good as anything else we offered. When I invited him
> to do some of the training he resisted, but I'm sure he felt
> pleased. We left it that we'd discuss it more next time. I didn't
> mind that because I wanted to see the other two first anyway. In
> fact, both of the others seemed easy in comparison. They had a
> lot of criticism about the training programme, but both agreed
> to get involved as long as we worked out a more convenient rota
> system and they had replacements where needed. They both
> said they would actually like to do some of the central training
> and I have fixed them into the programme. I'm certain that the
> first manager will now want to come in on the same basis. I think
> the difference was that I listened to them and was clearer with
> them about what I wanted to achieve.'

The others in the team reported on similar areas of communication
that they had had with their own managers, some noting real
improvements, others just reinforcing what was already good practice.

Chapter 5

Portfolios for Organization Development

If the portfolio approach for individual development is relatively new and, for team development, in its infancy, portfolio-building for organization development has hardly taken off. Yet for the training revolution to mean anything at all, its impact will have to be seen within organizations. The only time that individual and organization development is synonymous is within the one-person organization. Someone operating as a freelance interior designer working alone needs to develop his or her ideas and competence in order for the business to remain successful. As soon as other partners or staff become involved in the business, continued success depends on the whole team. In larger organizations there will be more teams, perhaps hundreds or even thousands of different teams. In those cases there is a bigger distance between the individual and the organization in terms of how each has impact on the other. The challenge for managers is how to reduce the gap.

This chapter will offer a process for organization development using a portfolio approach. It arises directly from the experience of working with a company that wanted to build itself into a learning organization. Much work had been done on learning organizations, notably by people like Pedlar, Burgoyne and Boydell in Britain and Argyris and Schon in the USA. Quality Circles and similar approaches had done much to assist companies in improving services and productivity. None of them, however, had really demonstrated that they had become learning organizations in the true sense. As defined by the Training Commission in Britain in 1988, a learning organization is 'an organization which facilitates the learning of all its members and continually transforms itself'.

The Sutcliffe Catering Group, a subsidiary of Granada, provides catering and other hotel services to nearly 2,000 organizations in Britain. These include offices, factories, schools, hospitals, ferries and residential establishments. In conjunction with the Employment Department, Sutcliffe wanted to test out an approach that could move it from being a company that prided itself on the training it provided for its 20,000 employees to being a learning company. As their training director at the time said, 'we've won the national training award, but as an organization we don't learn anything!'.

A programme called 'Learning from Experience' was set up in one of the company's profit centres, containing about 1,000 staff working in around 90 catering units. This section describes that programme as an illustration of how a portfolio approach can be used to develop an organization.

Aims

The central aim was 'to create a culture of learning within the profit centre and then to harness and share the learning in order to improve business performance at all levels'. The last part of the aim will be common to any organization, very few of whom would deny that they want to improve their performance in some way. Not so many will recognize that the first part of the aim is crucial to that performance.

The amount of potential learning that goes on within an organization is enormous. Most of us learn something new, however apparently trivial or irrelevant, every day. If we were encouraged to notice things more and ask more questions, we would learn even more. Instead, very little of what is learnt gets used or even heard about. Organizations must waste a vast amount of ideas and talent simply because there are so seldom any mechanisms for encouraging people to be aware of what goes on around them in the workplace and then for listening to them and valuing their contributions.

A pre-condition, therefore, for any successful learning organization is that it sets clear and committed aims for itself at the highest levels. An initiative recently launched by the Training and Enterprise Council (TEC) called 'Investors in People' takes up this theme by inviting employers to work towards a national standard. The standard has a set of four management principles:

An *Investor in People*
1. makes a public commitment from the top to develop all employees to achieve its business objectives;
2. regularly reviews the training and development needs of all employees;
3. takes action to train and develop individuals on recruitment and throughout their employment; and
4. evaluates the investment in training and development to assess achievement and improve future effectiveness.

In order to be recognized as an Investor in People, an organization has to be able to show how it plans to achieve those standards, and how it has reached them. While the emphasis is still on training rather than on learning, the initiative does seem to be making an impact on the thinking and the results within organizations. Before being awarded recognition, organizations must present a portfolio of evidence to show that they have met all the standard's requirements in full. It is interesting to see how one organization, already well versed in portfolio development, went about preparing themselves.

CCDU is a training, research and consultancy agency linked to the University of Leeds. In recent years they have worked with a number of organizations in helping them to design standards of competence for their own requirements. They have run programmes to assist individuals in developing their own portfolios and acted as assessors. CCDU have also had a policy of encouraging all their staff to develop through building their own portfolios.

In deciding to become an Investor in People, CCDU set up an action group which agreed the following principles:

1. The process is more important than the award.
2. The process is more important than achieving the award in a specified time.

3. Everyone in the organization must share in the process as well as in the outcomes.
4. The way we work to achieve the standard must mirror the standard itself.
5. We want things to be different and to have developed as a result of the process – as part of a strand of continuous improvement.
6. The action group must demonstrate their commitment by making this a priority.

These statements of principle indicate a mature organization and one which knows that it must establish its values before committing itself to a set of aims and objectives that may not be in line with what is acceptable and feasible for its own development. It was also part of a continual development process for CCDU rather than something which was a sudden and radical change to its culture.

Objectives/targets

Sutcliffe too was committed to ideals of development through a process of learning. The company's business, however, is very different from CCDU. Catering contractors work in a fast-moving and pressured environment with constant changes requested from customers, and one where staff is largely part time and highly mobile. Managers come from a variety of backgrounds, most of which are connected with the catering and leisure industry, where the idea of sharing ideas and learning from each other would be regarded as an unusual luxury. Such ideals and aims, therefore, are very difficult to 'sell' within the organization at all levels. Changing a culture may be one of the aims of portfolio development, but that takes time.

Most managers want clear, tangible objectives. In selling the idea of the Learning from Experience programme, the training director at Sutcliffe set such objectives and presented them to the managing director of the profit centre. They were both quantitative and qualitative. The quantitative ones were:

• to increase staff retention;

- to increase productivity;
- to reduce wastage;
- to reduce customer complaints; and
- to increase gross profits.

In each case, actual target figures were given. Qualitative objectives were:

- to gain innovative ideas from staff;
- to enhance customer awareness;
- to improve service to customers;
- to improve relationships and teamwork among staff; and
- to enable greater self-esteem and confidence among staff.

The objectives were accepted. The immediate implication of this was that figures had to be obtained on, for example, current staff retention and number of customer complaints. This in itself gave managers and staff a clearer picture of the position and what they needed to do to achieve their targets.

The boundaries of the learning organization

The ideal is that the whole of an organization is the learning unit. In reality, organizations are usually too large for that to happen in the shorter term. Since the essential factor is that everyone is involved, there is a need to define the boundaries that constitute the learning organization. In the case of Sutcliffe, it chose one particular profit centre because of its location, the extent to which existing training programmes had already begun to make some impact on the culture of the organization, and because its operations director was looking for ways to bring about changes in working patterns. Attempting to work across the whole of the company at this time would have been far too unwieldy and unrealistic.

Whatever the boundaries are, they must include the people who take the highest policy decisions as well as the ones who undertake the practical and administrative tasks at every level. In the Learning from Experience programme, Sutcliffe involved its top management and its cleaners and everyone in between of the 1,000 employees within the profit centre.

The process and programme

Sutcliffe's structure was the fairly traditionally hierarchical one for an organization of this nature. At the top of the profit centre was the operations director, accountable to the company's managing director. Reporting to the operations director were two general managers, each in charge of four areas. Each area had a manager who in turn was responsible for about ten unit managers who ran the catering units with an average of ten staff including chefs and general assistants.

At the higher levels managers already held regular meetings with their own teams: the operations manager with his general managers, the general managers with their area managers. Area managers tended to meet less regularly with their unit managers as a team. At unit level this seldom happened. Most meetings at any level were on the basis of information giving and problem solving.

The process for Learning from Experience was that every member of staff would be asked to keep a brief record of anything that came to their attention in connection with their work, ready to share this first with their manager or another colleague, then with the rest of their team. Team review meetings would be held regularly to share the items that had been noted and to agree what had been learnt and what action could be taken to change things if relevant. Anything learnt and anything to be changed would be taken by the manager to his or her own team meeting up or down the hierarchy.

The Learning from Experience programme included five key steps. These were:

1. **the briefing sessions;**
2. **portfolio material;**
3. **team review meetings;**
4. **sharing the learning; and**
5. **evaluating and disseminating the outcomes.**

1. The briefing sessions

The training director (who reported directly to the managing director) and the two consultants working with him, had briefing sessions with the operations director and his general managers and with the general managers and their area managers.

There were four parts to the briefing sessions. The first part outlined the aims of Learning from Experience. The second was practical, asking people to use the portfolio material that was provided for them. The third part was a demonstration of the team review process described in the previous chapter. The fourth part provided an opportunity for questions and a sharing of ideas.

During the briefing sessions a number of key points emerged. The first and most important one was the enthusiastic commitment of almost everyone to the idea – this, despite having been through several months of changes and working within a highly pressurized environment where it is easy to become cynical about management initiatives. The main reason was that those involved in the briefings had a positive experience for themselves, mirroring what we hoped would happen during the whole Learning from Experience process.

The second point to emerge was that there was a considerable number of issues and ideas that people wanted to share but had seldom had the chance. Most of those had arisen from experiences where the potential for positive learning and action could be seen. What commonly prevents such issues from being dealt with in a positive way is the lack of opportunity given to listening, coupled with the fear that people will only want to grumble at the manager.

Another factor was the apparent variation in the managers' ability in relation to facilitating a team in the way that would be required. Additional coaching would be needed for those people to work confidently and competently within a learning organization.

The final encouraging sign was that the Learning from Experience idea began in practice with the briefing sessions themselves. Not only were ideas and experiences shared, but action emerged from those early meetings that led to some practical and positive changes.

After the initial briefing sessions, most of the briefings of the unit managers' teams were done by the area managers and, with area managers' help when required, by the unit managers with their staff.

2. Portfolio material

Every member of staff was given a personal portfolio binder. It contained:

- a letter from the operations director;
- guidelines, with examples, for building a portfolio from experience;
- guidelines for helping someone else build a portfolio;
- copies of portfolio 'jotter pads'; and
- copies of team summary forms, with guidelines for team leaders.

Since the main aim of the process was portfolio-building for organization development, people were not asked to look at their previous learning, but to concentrate on immediate events and experiences in relation to their observations or their contact with their customer – whether this was an external or an internal customer.

After the initial dry run, the portfolio form itself was simplified in order to encourage as many people as possible to feel comfortable about using it. It asked four questions:

- what happened?
- what leads me to question what happened?
- what action do I need to take, or ideas do I have?
- who else should know about this?

Each person was asked to take a few minutes every day to note something. For most of those who were working as general assistants on the cash till, or cleaning and clearing up, work was seen as repetitive and mundane; for those working as managers it was often fraught with everyday problems. When people started to note things and then talk about them a change took place, not only in a practical sense but also in their own perception of what went on and what they could do. Here are some examples.

A unit manager wrote:

1. What happened?
   The client had asked for a buffet for their social club over the weekend. On Monday the social secretary complained that the buffet hadn't been what she'd expected. Yet she had simply asked

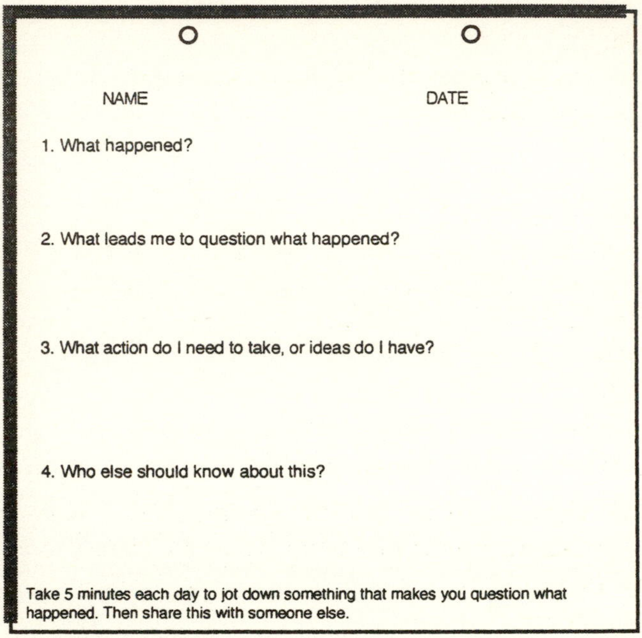

○   ○

NAME   DATE

1. What happened?

2. What leads me to question what happened?

3. What action do I need to take, or ideas do I have?

4. Who else should know about this?

Take 5 minutes each day to jot down something that makes you question what
happened. Then share this with someone else.

Figure 5.1 *The jotter pad portfolio from "Learning from Experience"*

the chef to prepare something to her budget and left it to his discretion.
2. What leads me to question what happened?
    *We have a set buffet menu. Didn't the chef show this to the client?
    The social secretary has often come to ask us to do something at
    very short notice and given little idea what she wants, then made
    a fuss about it. I need to know what the problem is.*
3. What action do I need to take, or ideas do I have?
    *I must talk to the chef and the social secretary and get to the bottom
    of this.*
4. Who else should know about this?
    *Nobody at this stage, but once I have spoken to the chef I may
    discuss this with the team.*

On the face of it, this seems to be an ordinary problem that can be
resolved at the unit level with few implications for anyone else, but
when the team met to discuss it later there were some valuable
lessons to be learnt and action to be taken.

A general assistant wrote:

1. What happened?
   When I worked on the till this week I noticed that not many people were buying salads. Last time I was on the till the salads went really well.
2. What leads me to question what happened?
   It's been really warm, so salads should have gone well. People didn't have the hot meals instead, they just took less.
3. What action do I need to take, or ideas do I have?
   I could ask people why they aren't having salads. I'll ask the manager if I can go on the till next week and tell her what I find out.
4. Who else should know about this?
   I'm not sure. I'll talk to the manager first.

Again, this seems an issue with little potential, certainly not for changing the organization. Once more, when this came to a team review meeting and action was taken there were significant implications for change.

An area manager wrote:

1. What happened?
   On the way in to work today, I noticed that the office block that has been vacant for two years appears to have been rented.
2. What leads me to question what happened?
   If someone has just taken over that block, there might be an opening for us that's worth investigating.
3. What action do I need to take, or ideas do I have?
   I'll try to find out if the offices have been let, and if so to whom. Maybe they are a potential client. I'll tell my general manager what I find out and discuss how to approach them.
4. Who else should know about this?
   I should think the operations director. But I'll talk to my boss first.

In each case, the individuals who had noted something discussed it with their line managers, then took the issue to their own team review. Some people talked informally with their staff colleagues before taking it forward. Sometimes it was enough to leave it there, because small though significant changes could take place there and then.

3. Team review meetings

Given the kind of operation run by Sutcliffe, team review meetings were run on a hierarchical basis and varied in frequency, length and style. The most successful ones were those where the process mirrored those held during the briefing. The size of the group depended on the team. At unit level, the numbers varied from six to twelve and included all the staff, most of whom were part time, plus the unit manager and sometimes the area manager. There were about 90 such teams. At area level, the team consisted of around ten area managers plus the general manager. There were two such teams, although because of distance it often happened that a general manager would meet with half of the team in two different locations. The operations director met with the two general managers, and also sometimes with an area team.

It was at the team review where people actually had a chance to write something into their jotter pad if they had not already done so. Some people came prepared; others, usually those unused to writing anything, needed a little time and encouragement. Once it became clear that they really could write down even an apparently mundane experience, and that nobody else would be reading it anyway, people felt more comfortable about what they wrote.

Once everyone at the team review had had the chance to reflect on and jot down an experience, they were asked to meet in pairs for five or ten minutes to share what they had got. This ensured that everyone had an opportunity to hear what someone else had to say and to be listened to.

The manager, acting as the team leader and facilitator, then invited one of the team to share the experience that he or she had recorded. The process used was the seven-step group dialogue described in the previous chapter. The portfolio binders included team summary forms so that everyone could note down what had been discussed and what action had been agreed. In other words, everyone had the responsibility of ensuring that things were noted, although it was the specific responsibility of the person who had raised the issue to follow things up. Here are the outcomes from the team reviews of each of the three examples I gave earlier.

The unit manager read out his notes to his own staff in their team review, then went on to say:

I spoke to the chef who confirmed that the client had come in late on Thursday to request a buffet for a function that had been hurriedly switched to this venue. Chef told me that the social secretary had said she had a tight budget and that the buffet we'd had last time would be all right. Chef had shown her our menu, and she had pointed to one, asked for 90 meals and rushed out. When I called her on Friday to confirm the arrangements she had said that she had no time to discuss it but was happy to leave it to us.

As a result of the dialogue, the following action was agreed:

The chef and the unit manager will arrange for photographs to be taken of a variety of buffet meals and put into a display menu. This can be circulated around their offices with the client's approval.

The unit manager will arrange to meet the social secretary, discuss with her the ideas for the buffet meals and photos and ask her for suggestions. Regular contact will be kept with her so that a better relationship is established for the future.

The unit manager will take the idea for the photographed buffet meals to the next unit managers' team review and discuss it with them and the area manager as an idea.

The action was taken; the client and the chef were both delighted with the results and there were no more complaints.

The general assistant reported to her team review and added:

When I told the manager she agreed that I go back on the till. We worked out a questionnaire and I handed it to everyone who came that week. Most people answered it, probably because I asked them to. At the end of the first two days it was obvious what the problem was. They said that the salad selection hadn't changed and they wanted more variety.

The dialogue resulted in the following action:

The chef would prepare different selections of salads on each day. Whoever was on the till would monitor the sale of particular dishes, especially the salads.

A questionnaire would be done every three months to assess customer satisfaction.

The unit manager would report to her area manager and team.

The action was taken. Salad sales shot up dramatically. So did customer satisfaction.

The area manager who had noticed the office block rented out shared this with the team. The review revealed the following information:

The company who had taken up the offices were a subsidiary of a current client in another part of the country.
They planned to be moving in within two months and would be seeking a catering contractor.

The following action was agreed:

The general manager will prepare a feasibility report and discuss this with the operations director and area manager.
The area manager will contact the potential client to discuss his requirements.
The general manager will prepare a tender on the basis of the discussions.

The action was taken, the tender was successful and a new unit was set up in the area manager's area.

4. Sharing the learning

Portfolios for organization development mean that the learning and action that takes place in one team must be transferred to the other teams up, down and across the hierarchy. In an ideal world there would be no barriers to communication. A young, new trainee office worker with a good idea, or an experienced sales manager concerned with changing fashions, would have equal access to the managing director or anyone else in the organization. Since it seldom works like that, for logistical as well as reasons to do with the maintenance of status, we need to find systems to improve organization communication and learning.

In the Learning from Experience case study, Sutcliffe managers at all levels took the main issues that arose from the team reviews with their staff to their own peer review team which included their manager. Similarly, issues from one review would be taken by a member to the team that he or she managed. As result, ideas and information were spread more effectively around the organization.

The three examples show the kinds of practical results that accrued.

At an area managers' review, one area manager showed her team's portfolio that included photographs of the buffet selection and how communication had been improved with the unit's client. The following action was agreed:

The area manager would circulate the illustrated menus to all units and to the other area managers for their use as appropriate.

The importance of keeping regular communication with key people within the client's premises was emphasized through this experience. Each area manager would ask unit managers to identify those key people and ensure that they made at least informal contact with them at agreed regular intervals.

At a unit managers' review, the experience of increasing salad sales was given. The resultant action was:

Unit managers would encourage their staff to ask more questions of customers when they noticed any change in buying patterns.

Regular customer satisfaction forms, tailored to the particular unit and conditions, to be given to customers on a quarterly basis.

Chefs to be encouraged to put more variety into menus and presentation.

The general assistant who came up with the idea to be given a special award.

At the general managers' review with the operations director, the instance of the potential client was explored. The action was:

The general managers to relay this experience at their area managers' review and encourage them to look for similar opportunities.

The area manager who initiated the action to be kept closely involved with the progress of the new contract at every step.

The operations director to inform the managing director of the new contract as one of the more significant outcomes of Learning from Experience.

5. Evaluating and disseminating the outcomes

In a sense, the whole process is one of continual evaluation and dissemination. Into everyone's portfolio goes his or her own everyday experience, learning and action; the outcomes and decisions taken by the team in relation to their own experience; and the feedback people get about their own performance. In the cases given, some of the evidence that went into portfolios is given here.

The unit manager put into his portfolio:

- the photos of the buffet meals with the menus;
- a schedule of the times noted to see the social secretary and other key people;
- the notes of the situation that led to this;
- a copy of the memo that went to all unit managers circulating the photos; and
- a letter from the social secretary thanking the staff for the buffet served at a social event four months later.

The chef had similar items in his portfolio.

The general assistant put into her portfolio:

- notes of what she had seen and the action agreed;
- copies of the questionnaire she had helped to produce;
- a copy of the letter from the area manager; and
- a breakdown of the sales of items showing the increase since her idea was implemented.

The area manager put into his portfolio:

- a photo of the office block with notes about his observations;
- notes from the team review when the action was agreed;
- invitations from the general manager and operations director to discuss the matter;
- a letter to the prospective client;
- a copy of the feasibility study with notes by the area manager;
- a copy of the tender; and
- a copy of the contract and letter of acceptance from the client.

As well as the continuing evaluation and dissemination of the outcomes through the process of portfolio-building, there needs to

be an overall evaluation. For that, the organization must go back
to its originally stated aims and objectives.

For Sutcliffe's, the aim was:

> 'to create a culture of learning within the profit centre and then
> to harness and share the learning in order to improve business
> performance at all levels.'

The objectives were:

> to increase staff retention
> to increase productivity
> to reduce wastage
> to reduce customer complaints
> to increase gross profits

all to specified target figures. In addition, qualitative objectives
were:

> to gain innovative ideas from staff
> to enhance customer awareness
> to improve service to customers
> to improve relationships and teamwork among staff
> to enable greater self-esteem and confidence among staff

Whether or not longer term aims of this nature are achieved
depends on how much commitment remains at the top of an
organization and how much this is passed on and sustained through
all levels and by new staff coming in, especially at the top. Changes
in the structure at Sutcliffe were both helped by Learning from
Experience and served to hinder its progress.

The shorter term objectives are easier to see. At Sutcliffe they
were all achieved, some beyond all expectation:

- Staff retention was the most dramatic achievement. Contract catering has a traditionally high staff turnover, especially among part-time staff. During the first year of
  Learning from Experience, staff turnover dropped from 98
  per cent overall, to 22 per cent!
- Productivity was increased by over 5 per cent.
- Wastage was reduced by 5–10 per cent.

- Customer complaints dropped by nearly 15 per cent.
- Gross profits increased, even in a time of general downturn.

More difficult to evaluate are the qualitative targets. Some can be counted; others can be identified by comments from staff, for example during or after team review sessions:

- Staff certainly came up with more innovative ideas than ever before.
- Staff throughout the profit centre appeared much more aware of the customers.
- Service to customers improved, seen by the attention they felt they now received.
- Relationships and teamwork among staff improved significantly. The team review sessions gave people a real sense of involvement for the first time in what went on.
- Self-esteem and confidence among staff increased. Many of the staff had never spoken out at any meeting, and certainly not written anything down. Their portfolios and their participation in team reviews showed their own development.

The training director, in evaluating the success of Learning from Experience after it had run for a year, noted that:

'significant success was achieved in some parts of the profit centre where a new spirit of empowerment and free contribution was fostered. . . . The main success of the project was, in several areas, the demonstration of how simple it is for working groups to become effective teams in terms of learning, sharing and developing their business. Where groups realized that the process was in no way manipulative and was intended to bring about employee-led change rather than adherence to company norms, the programme succeeded.'

Needless to say, not everyone in an organization of 1,000 people will find it easy to accept a process that overturns a lifetime habit of being taught or being told by superiors what do to and how to do things. Nor will all those who have attained positions of authority find it palatable to give up some of their methods of asserting their power. Even where people feel secure and positive enough to work in the way I have described, there will be barriers. Time and attention need to be invested in this process for it to work fully.

The Sutcliffe training director wrote:

'a pitfall, which could have been anticipated, was the threat felt by certain managers that arose from, as they saw it, a more participative or collective style of management. As learning meetings were always chaired by the immediate supervisor of the learning group, there was an implicit risk to that supervisor's sovereignty. Less autocratic and more secure managers did not find this to be any obstacle. . . . Despite largely successful attempts to prevent it from happening, some still saw it to do with training rather than learning and as an attempt to detect and correct errors, rather than a process that would encourage change, innovation and personal development'.

Evaluating the process

The outcomes of Learning from Experience were written up and published, complete with a video to illustrate the process, by Sutcliffe Catering Group in collaboration with the Employment Department Learning Technologies Unit and made available to other organizations who wanted to explore a similar process. The pack includes guidelines for managers and organizations and a description of the case study as well as the video.

Some of the key pre-conditions for success that were identified are:

1. the process needs to be introduced by people who have had value out of the same process themselves – it therefore needs to originate and be supported from above;
2. the process is seen to be simple and pragmatic;
3. the outcomes of the learning are actions that are implemented and reviewed and found to be successful;
4. communication is seen to be vertical as well as horizontal;
5. new staff at all levels are quickly inducted into the process; and
6. the process becomes an automatic part of the organization's

culture and sufficient time needs to be allowed for the process to take root.

The organization guidelines concluded that the successful learning organization needs to have or develop a structure that enables:

1. staff at any level to communicate upwards, downwards and across the hierarchy;
2. managers to encourage the process of sharing informally with individuals and within more formal team meetings;
3. information and ideas on good practice to be shared quickly throughout the organization;
4. outcomes of the process to be fed into formal decision-making procedures (eg board meetings); and
5. originators of ideas/good practice to be recognized.

The managers' guidelines in the pack also include some suggestions for getting started. Since you might like to use this yourself, the suggestions are reproduced here.

How Learning from Experience works in your organization will depend upon your own circumstances and what is agreed to be the best approach. From our own experience, we suggest the following steps:

1. Try it yourself. The importance of this cannot be overemphasized. You should be introduced to the process by your own manager (unless you're the boss) and you in turn should introduce it to your staff team. Nobody should be asked to be involved until the person asking has tried it and found it worth while.
2. Look at the jotter pad accompanying this package. There are four questions on each page of the jotter pad. [See Figure 5.1.] Give it a try now.
3. Then discuss what you have written with a colleague.
4. If there is some action to take as a result of your thoughts and discussion, take it; or talk it over with whoever is appropriate; ideally with the team of people who are most closely affected by any changes.
5. When you are ready, introduce the idea to members of your staff and ask them to try it out in the same way.
6. Set a regular time, say once a week for 30 minutes, especially to share some of the ideas that individuals have thought about, or to consider the questions that they have to ask from what they have experienced during the past few days.

The final word on the Sutcliffe case study should come from the training director.

'The main conclusions drawn were that learning and contributing are natural parts of individuals' lives and simply need a culture (and system) for encouraging them to happen. However, it also became clear that the organization itself needs to be managed in order to allow learning to take place, and many of the inherent barriers of hierarchy and traditional working practices need to be removed for the full benefit of learning to be derived.'

Portfolios for organization development, then, present a real challenge to management; but the rewards can be enormous.

A framework for portfolio development in organizations

As with portfolios for personal and professional development, and portfolios for team development, there are five key steps to be taken at an organizational level to ensure that the whole process is integrated. The five steps are:

1. **Values and aims (why are we doing this?)**
2. **Human resources (who have we got?)**
3. **Needs analysis (what have they got and what do they need?)**
4. **Development plan (how can we provide the learning structure?)**
5. **Organization review (how have we done; what can we change?)**

Each of those steps in the framework is, as with the whole portfolio process, continual since they are built into the structure once it is set up. Organizations who already take pride in their own development programmes will find that this simply enhances what they have. Those who wish to explore how they can develop into more of a learning organization can take on the processes described here.

1. Values and aims (why are we doing this?)

Any organization must take a look from time to time at why it works in the way it does. Even the most successful companies do this, which is probably why they stay the most successful companies. Those who have been successful in the past and ridden on that success without bothering to look at what is going on around them and without asking themselves some key questions, have recently found themselves suddenly having to make drastic and painful changes.

In seeking to become a learning organization and developing through a portfolio approach, those at the highest levels in any organization must be clear about their values and what they are aiming to achieve. Those things can include quantitive aspects like profit margins and good salaries. They can also include the qualitative things like happy customers, people who take a pride in their work, confident and satisfied staff, and opportunities for everyone to develop themselves. Companies who have worked towards a mission statement will know how hard it can be to finish up with such apparently simple statements. Apart from the overall values, the organization needs to be clear about its aims for the future. What is the direction the organization wants to take; what precisely does it want to achieve over the next two or three years?

2. Human resources (who have we got?)

The next question for the organization to consider is what resources it has and what it needs to get where it wants to be. The portfolio approach concentrates on the human resources and the most important question is: who have you got now? The question is not just about the numbers, functions and names of personnel, but what have those people got to contribute? What are their strengths? How do you find out?

In the portfolio work I have done and heard about over the past few years, I have constantly heard surprise expressed when people discover the skills and experience of others who sometimes have been working colleagues for years. Harnessing even a fraction of those strengths can transform activities and the people who perform them.

3. Needs analysis (what competences are needed?)

This stage has recently become dramatically easier since it has been recognized that all work can be carried out to a recognized set of quality standards. The training revolution has seen many industries and professions develop those standards from core competences to the performance indicators that can show whether or not somebody has demonstrated those competences.

Organizations throughout the UK can now use those standards as a way of defining what skills and knowledge they require in order for them to achieve their objectives. Where standards are not yet in place, or are not particularly relevant, an organization can relatively easily define its own standards using NVQs as a model.

Once an organization has determined what it needs, remembering that this will change as circumstances change, it can relate this to what strengths staff already have. The gap between what is needed and what is demonstrated provides the information on what competences still need to be developed.

This is very different from a one-off training audit. Using portfolios for organization development will give continual information about where there are weaknesses that need to be addressed and where there are strengths that can be used more productively.

4. Development plan (how can we provide the learning structure?)

The success or otherwise of the portfolio approach in a learning organization lies with whoever decides on its policy and has the task of overseeing it in practice. Having gained the information through the process itself – of defining aims, human resources and the strengths needed and available – a plan can be developed to ensure that learning opportunities are put into place.

Most learning and new competences are best gained through actual experience. Any development plan needs to examine the optimum way for this to take place within the work environment. How can people try out new skills? How can they discover what happens in other parts of the organization? How can they learn different ways of doing things; and unlearn some bad habits? How can this take place in the workplace to best advantage and without causing disruption?

Who are the people who could provide the learning within work? One of the most valuable learning opportunities is for someone to be given the task of teaching others. So the next question is: how can those people gain the skills of facilitating learning? Similarly, one of the key roles of any manager in the portfolio approach is to act as group facilitator in the team review sessions. Every manager needs this ability, portfolios or not. Since it is positively required in this approach, that is another compelling reason to consider the process.

Sometimes the most appropriate way for people to learn is by going on formal training courses, either away from the organization or with other members of staff in the work setting. Far too often the training course is seen by managers as a way of dealing with staff who are a problem to them. Increasingly, the appraisal system is used as a way of defining the relevant training. This is an improvement, although in larger organizations it can take a year or more before the person gets on the training course. More problematically, the training course may not be the right one, or not the appropriate learning medium. Moreover, the follow-up at work from training courses is usually non-existent, with the result that much valuable learning is not used inside the organization.

Training targeted to real learning needs and followed up within the workplace, however, can be very effective. The portfolio approach helps to ensure this. If the development plan includes the processes I have described here and allows for managers and staff to have the competences required to carry out the approach, people who have been on a training course will be able to share this as an experience in their next team review. Their portfolio will enable them to put new ideas and skills into action with the help of their supervisor.

5. Organization review (how have we done; what can we change?)

You don't have to wait for a year or two before reviewing how the organization has done and how, in retrospect, you would have changed things if only you had given it another year. Certainly

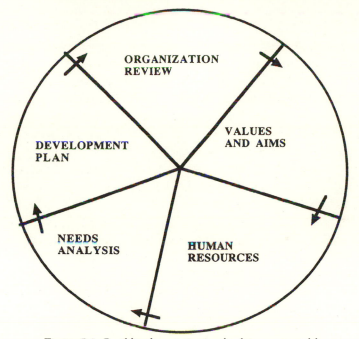

Figure 5.2 *Portfolios for organization development: a model*

there are likely to be set targets that can only be evaluated properly after a reasonable period has elapsed. Changes taking place as a result of the portfolio process, however, can be seen almost immediately.

Questions for the organization can arise where it is seen that those changes are taking place for the better in some parts, or some departments, rather than in others. The feedback that comes in as an integral part of the process enables a quick recognition of where things are working well and where they are not. Where things work, people can be acknowledged and their efforts reinforced. Where nothing much seems to be happening, action can be taken to find out why it's not and what can be done about it.

Reasons for people not learning and making positive changes to working practices are likely to be: a lack of time, coupled with too much reactive work going on; poorly run team review meetings, or no team reviews; no encouragement for people to record and talk about their experiences; lack of mentors; few opportunities given for learning; and no doubt many others. All of those reasons are cause for concern in any organization. Through the portfolio approach they can be detected and highlighted for action on a continuing basis. Customer complaints and reduced productivity do not have to be the only reasons for making changes.

Chapter 6

A Model for Portfolio Development

We can now look at how to integrate personal and professional (individual) development with team and organization development. We have looked at three separate models so far. It is possible for the individual model to stand on its own and for individuals to develop, with assistance, by going through the learning processes described. The team development model is likely to be successful only if it relates to the individual development process. The organization development model has little meaning without the other two.

In this chapter I will explore how each of the phases of each model interrelates with the other two and describe how this can work in practice.

First, here is a reminder of the phases of each of the three portfolio development models, not necessarily in the order they were given.

Individual	Team	Organization
Experience	Team review	Organization review
Learning	Appraisal	Values and aims
Demonstration	Strengths	Human resources
Learning needs	Competences	Needs analysis
Learning opportunities	Action and training	Development plan

The model may look rather complicated at this stage but we will

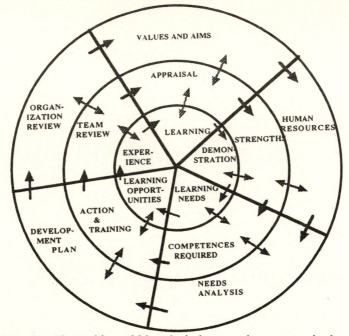

Figure 6.1 *The portfolio model for individual, team and organization development*

unravel it in this chapter. The inner circle on the model represents the portfolio learning cycle for individual development; the middle circle represents the stages of team development; and the outer circle, organization development. The model shows how crucial the team is, both to individuals and the organization. It is within the team that individuals can offer and gain ideas and information; and through teams that the organization can communicate its plans and discover what is going on.

Taking each segment of the model in turn, we can see the impact each has on the other. I will look at the individual's development process first, then the team's and finally the organization's. It is the organization, that is to say the individuals at the highest levels of decision-taking, that must start the process by putting everything into place; but there will be no organization development unless all the individuals develop.

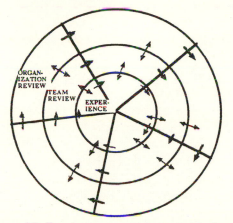

Figure 6.2 *Experience – team review – organization review*

Experience – team review – organization review

The individual – experience

The starting point for the individual is the opportunity to explore the range of experience that he or she has. This may be prior experience of a very broad nature or it may be current, everyday experience specific to a particular activity. The first step in looking at prior experience is the index; the second step is to tell the story of each of the experiences. The recorded material goes into the individual's portfolio.

The team – team review

The place where the individual can share his or her experience and listen to others is, in this model, through the team review. Where provision is made for teams to gather regularly – not to go through a managerially imposed agenda, but to enable people to share their experiences – they will learn to value what they have done and take a pride in observing what goes on and bringing their ideas to the team.

The team review will not only hear what individuals within that team have done; it will also take that information through other parts of the organization, up, down and across the hierarchy. This means that the experience gained by one person and taken to one team, will soon be taken to the top management team in the organization where it has implications for them.

In one shoe factory, trying out this process some years ago, an operative whose task was to scour the bottom of the leather upper before the sole was fixed, noticed that on a new design there was a danger of the pattern being damaged. He brought this to the attention of the team leader and they agreed to hold up that design and keep the production line going with others. The next morning there was a brief team review when the problem was raised. Immediate action was agreed to take this to the production manager. In the late afternoon, a team review was held of the team leaders with the production manager. A design fault was established and rectified. Had the shoes continued through the production line it would have cost the company many thousands of pounds.

Of course, anyone would say, this is all obvious. Nobody would let such a fault go by. Yet this same factory, only months before, had been letting such apparently minor slips go through, unnoticed by anybody except the customers, who sent back over 1,000 pairs of shoes. The cost – in terms of actual loss in profit from returned and faulty goods, plus the loss of a customer (who never came back) and the loss of confidence of staff in their own product – was incalculable to this small factory. The fact was that nobody cared, because nobody asked anything of anyone, or thought that they had anything to offer apart from getting on with their mostly boring and repetitive jobs.

Within two weeks of setting up a process for portfolio development, the company saved a lot of money, gave staff at all levels a much greater feeling of ownership and responsibility, and over the following months helped change the whole atmosphere from one of gloom and dismay to a lighter, more confident workplace in which success seemed possible.

The organization – organization review

Using the portfolio process means that the organization is under constant review. At the level of top decision making, the senior managers get regular feedback from their immediate reports through their own team reviews and can take this information into the board room. The information that is coming in at this stage relates to people's experience right through the organization. Here is the biggest challenge of all.

Will the senior management team be courageous enough to put into practice for itself what it is advocating for the rest of the organization? This is where much of the potential for change falls down.

In the shoe factory, in the first months of setting up this process the directors had listened to what was being discovered and decided that significant changes in middle management practices needed to be made. People throughout the factory became more in control of their own departments and functions, with the team leaders concerning themselves much more with planning and pro-active quality control. The directors themselves were faced with changing their own responsibilities and becoming more staff- and market-conscious. All this had come about because a new director had been brought in to assist in turning around the company's declining business performance. Unfortunately a majority of the board was uncomfortable with the changes they were having to make and slid back into their old autocratic ways with the classic statement 'people on the shop floor are much happier being told what to do'. Two years later the company went into liquidation.

The organization review, therefore, takes place everywhere but needs to be acted upon at the highest levels. Most important of all, decisions made at a review need to be communicated through the rest of the organization. People must know that they are having an impact in order to maintain the motivation for the process.

Learning – appraisal – values and aims

The individual – learning

Learning is an individual process. It may be derived from experience, but experience in itself does not guarantee that learning will follow. What the portfolio process can offer is little more than an opportunity for people to discover more about themselves and their work from their experience. What it does do is to make learning a natural and consistent part of what goes on, rather than it

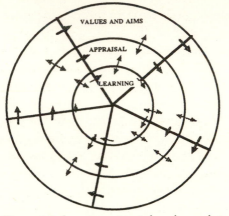

Figure 6.3 *Learning – appraisal – values and aims*

being set aside as a specialist activity for those who are seen as
worthy recipients.

Regular and considered reflection on events, recorded by the
individual who has been a part of them, is a powerful tool for
self-learning and understanding. Supported by a structure and with
the help of a mentor and others, learning becomes as natural to the
adult as it was to the child. Much of the subsequent years of growth,
including formal education, has stunted our capacity to continue
the learning process.

The team – appraisal

Appraisal has become used as a management tool increasingly over
the last few years. Sometimes it is used positively, sometimes neg-
atively. The intentions are almost always presented in a positive
light; it is to do with improving performance, getting people to see
how they are viewed by their managers, rewarding excellence and
so on.

In the portfolio approach, appraisal is seen to operate most effectively and positively within the context of the team. The two key
questions of the appraisal, 'what have we gained?' and 'what's
next?', when linked to individual and organization become 'what
has this person learnt from the experience that we have shared?'
and 'how are the values and aims of the organization being fur-
thered by this person's performance?'

The team becomes the place where individual and organization communicate with each other. The organization discovers what its individuals have learnt about their work and about the organization. The individual is confronted by the values espoused by the organization and by having to ask whether he or she has helped to achieve its aims.

One local government department was confronted with the requirement to set up an appraisal system. There was resistance from staff, who saw it as a reduction of their professionalism and feared that managers would deal with it in an authoritarian way. In discussion, staff and management agreed that appraisal would be carried out within teams through a system of self and peer appraisal, with regular reports to the manager. A 12 months' trial period was given for this procedure, in the face of considerable disquiet from the manager of the department.

The team of 12 people met to decide how they would go about the appraisal. They agreed on the following procedure:

- Each person would write down what his or her objectives had been for the previous six months and how those reflected the department's aims.
- A set of key, common questions was formulated for the appraisal.
- The team would meet in groups of three: one person to assist another in reviewing what he or she had done, learnt and achieved over the previous period; the third person just to observe the process and give feedback at the end. Each person would take on each of those three roles in turn.
- At the end of each appraisal session (only one session took place at a time, so the group of three met on three occasions), each person being appraised would record what he or she had said.
- When the appraisals had been completed the whole team would meet, with their manager, to review the process and to submit their findings; at that meeting the manager would be asked to respond and to give his views on the appraisal process.

As part of the agreement the team undertook some training in appraisal interviewing, made relevant to their own needs.

The procedure was completed twice. The subsequent evaluation was so positive that it was adopted throughout the organization.

The organization – values and aims

The processes within the portfolio approach do not take place synchronously; the setting of an organization's values and aims takes place over a period of time. Values change only over a long period; aims perhaps every five to ten years in some organizations. Other organizations will set different aims more frequently when they are in a faster moving field, or are smaller, more flexible and wanting to respond more quickly to clients.

Once a complete portfolio process is running, the organization will be in a position to reassess its values and aims and to communicate them on a regular basis. Through the information that senior management obtains as a result of the teams' appraisal, a clearer and quicker appreciation can be made of the extent to which its values are in line with what is needed and whether the aims are in fact the ones that are appropriate. Many organizations are seen as being distant from their customers. Governments and public service organizations are regularly accused of this. This is partly to do with their size; however, that is largely an excuse for inaccessible management who do not set up an adequate communication system within their organization.

In the local government department that set up a peer appraisal system, the outcomes were more far-reaching than they had at first imagined. The team of 12 demonstrated that not only could they be trusted to carry out their own peer appraisal, but that they were probably more rigorous in their own analysis and more determined to enhance their work than would have been the case had the appraisal been carried out under more traditional methods. When the results of the trial period were taken by the manager to his own senior management team meeting, this caused considerable interest.

The senior managers decided to discover precisely what had happened and what the practical results had been. They found that the departmental team had set up its own process, had carried it out and had reported back regularly. Programme planning had improved, targets had been set and achieved, new projects were being developed at a faster pace than before, and the team had put together a proposal for an improved induction training programme for new staff. The managers were also confronted with questions from the team who wanted clearer organization guidelines on broader issues. The senior managers, faced with this information and the questions, took the bold step of going through the same peer appraisal system among themselves. Once they had evaluated this, they met and made the following statement:

> 'We believe that our people are our most valued resources. We intend to demonstrate that belief by encouraging all staff to take responsibility for ensuring that they carry out their duties in the most effective way they can, and learn constantly how to improve on their own efforts. We will support a system of peer group appraisal, where everyone will both give and receive support from colleagues. In the same way that we desire to give a good service to all our clients, we wish to provide a good management service to our staff. This means that we will listen to them and expect them to tell us about their work and their contact with the community we serve.'

The organization had defined some values and aims as a result of discovering what people had learnt, and had communicated those values and aims for people to test against their own work.

Demonstration – strengths – human resources

The individual – demonstration

The centrepiece of the individual's portfolio is the demonstration or the proof of his or her competence in a given area of work. This may be set against a specific standard when looking at awarding accreditation, or it may stand in its own right as a piece of evidence of that person's development – 'I couldn't do that before, and I can now'.

We have looked at the kind of things that can go into an individual's portfolio to record the proof of competence. Once in the portfolio, the individual can use it as a piece of self-knowledge for personal satisfaction, or it can be presented to an assessor as part

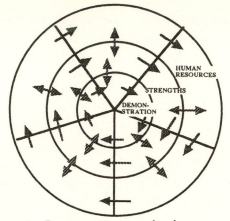

Figure 6.4 *Demonstration – strengths – human resources*

of an accreditation procedure, or it may be shared with a team of people as part of a wider development process.

The team – strengths

I once worked in an organization with about 20 other professionals, including social workers, health specialists, educationalists and trainers. Although I worked with some of them quite closely for about three years, we knew each other only in our professional capacities. Not long before I left, about a dozen of us became involved in a programme that would mean us working together in different ways on a theme that few of us had much experience in: researching, developing and writing about new ways of working with disadvantaged young people in community settings.

At our initial planning meeting, we decided that, if we were to be effective in moulding ourselves as a cohesive unit, we should see what our joint strengths were. Everyone was asked to spend five minutes saying what he or she brought to the group, with no boundaries on the kind of experiences we could share. One of us wrote up on a flipchart the strengths identified.

Apart from the ones we knew about – the professional skills that we brought overtly to our work – the list included the following:

leader in a jazz band

had run a school in Papua New Guinea
edited travel guides
produced and directed stage plays
had fostered eight children
ran a youth centre
had sailed the Atlantic in a crew of six
spent two years in hospital with a life-threatening illness
involved in local politics
marriage guidance counsellor
wrote short stories for magazines
had built own house extension

We were all amazed at the sum total of our strengths – all discovered in the space of 20 minutes. None of us had any idea about most of these; we had simply not given ourselves the opportunity to find out. But did it help us to be more effective as a team? When we explored the actual abilities that we could combine, we saw that between us we could demonstrate:

leadership and organizing skills in a range of areas
team skills
writing and editing skills
knowledge and understanding of young people
patience, energy, durability and determination
speaking and negotiating skills
listening and counselling skills
practical skills

The individual demonstrations of competence are the aggregate of the strengths of the team. The implication is that not everyone needs to have all the competences required for the team to perform well. Inevitably, some people will be better at some things than others. Rather than having to bring everyone up to the same standard, it may well be more productive to use what is there creatively. From the appraisal process within a team, it is an easy step to share the strengths. The leader needs to be able to put those together and to present them back to the team.

There are two next steps. One is to feed the information into other parts of the organization; the other is to establish the overall competences required to undertake the work in hand.

The organization – human resources

The smaller the organization, the easier it would seem to establish what it has in terms of human resources. As my example just now has shown, even in an organization of 20 people something has to happen before we can really find out what exists. A system must be put into place.

Where individuals are empowered to demonstrate their competences and where teams are encouraged to share their strengths, the organization can answer the question 'who have we got?' by ensuring that the information is fed through the system. Managers at all levels have to show an interest in the qualities of their staff. There is an overemphasis on what people can't or don't do, so we work to their weaknesses rather than draw out their strengths.

At the highest level of management, where organizational policy is developed, there needs to be a system that enables corporate strengths to be known and acknowledged. After all, customers would want to know about those too, and would want to see them manifested.

Learning needs – competences required – needs analysis

The individual – learning needs

This is the stage of ownership – when the person who has demonstrated competence also defines and accepts responsibility for what he or she still needs to learn. This is far easier to do when first, the individual has been able to give proof of personal abilities, and second, when others are going through the same process and it is part of the acknowledged way of doing things.

In a culture where admission of imperfection is regarded as an unacceptable weakness and where a questioning approach is seen as stupidity, people will not want to admit or take any responsibility for learning needs. In organizations where the portfolio approach is seen as a way forward, empowerment will already be a theme.

The individual at this stage will be asking two questions in order to establish his or her learning needs. The first will be:

'what additional skills or knowledge do I want for myself now or in the future to be able to do what I want to do?'

The second is:

'what does the organization (employer, accreditation body etc) require of me now and in the future apart from the competences I can already demonstrate?'

This second question, especially, means that there needs to be an interaction between the individual and the organization even where the portfolio-building is purely a personal task.

The team – competences required

The transition from the team sharing its joint strengths to identifying the competences required for it to carry out its work well, is a straightforward one, as long as there is adequate communication with others in the organization. Again, the team is in the middle of the communication between individual and organization.

Managers of teams need the information and the skills to be able to conduct the process effectively. The team leader, in consultation with team members and, where relevant, their mentors, will have established personal learning goals and contracts. There will also have been a recognition of overall competences within the

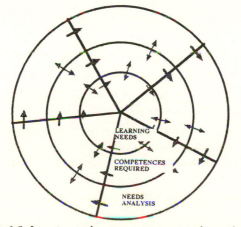

Figure 6.5 *Learning needs – competences required – needs analysis*

team. All this must now be put against the objectives and targets set for the group over the coming period.

Will there be new forms of work; or new technology; or additional staff brought in; or different standards required? All these and other considerations will lead the team to explore the competences needed and to define where new ones must be gained. There may be individuals who will wish to develop new skills, or the team as a whole might work together to raise its overall performance.

In the team I described earlier, where we had discovered many hitherto hidden talents, we found that we would need to set up a number of conferences and develop good working contacts with the media. We also wanted to make ourselves familiar with some new legislation that could affect our work. None of us felt confident enough to take on either of the first two tasks and we agreed that we should all know about the legislation. Two of our number would gain the skills needed in setting up and running conferences, while another would develop the knowledge and skills in working with the media. Another undertook to convene a seminar for all of us and invite someone to lead it who was knowledgeable about the legal aspects.

The organization – needs analysis

It would be a potential waste of energy and time for each team to decide in isolation on what competences were needed and then to take the necessary action. There is a lot to commend that practice; nevertheless, the organization may have many teams, all identifying similar things and replicating each other's action.

More than that, the organization's leaders need to have an overview, or the 'helicopter vision' that enables them to assess what is needed ahead of time. They must make an analysis of the human (among other) resources that will be needed and ensure that they are in place when they are required. Many organizations already have sophisticated human resource planning mechanisms to make sure that people are there when they are needed. Few have an ongoing system that provides for an exchange of information between staff and senior managers on what is wanted and what is available in order for people to establish their own learning needs.

Learning opportunities – action and training – development plan

The individual – learning opportunities

The time for real growth for the individual is when he or she embarks upon a self-managed learning programme. The more the team and the organization is involved, the wider will be the learning opportunities offered and the greater the incentive to learn and to change things.

Trainers often justify much of the work they ask their trainees to do as 'providing learning opportunities'. They go further and say that almost anything that happens, on or off the training course, is another learning opportunity. The trouble is that a learning opportunity is only as good as the motivation and ability of the person to use it as such.

The provision of a learning opportunity, therefore, is much more potent when the learner has asked for one and had at least a hand in devising what it should be. This takes place within a well-run portfolio process. The individual has been through the stages that brings him or her to negotiate a learning contract and is supported by others in the team.

Once taken up, the completed learning stage goes back into the individual's portfolio as another experience, which can be demonstrated as a new competence.

The team – action and training

Learning is an active process. This means that action has to be taken to enable it to take place. The team's role within a portfolio process is to support and challenge the individuals within it to take on the appropriate action.

It may well be relevant to set up a training programme formally. In the case of our team, we had a day seminar with someone who had the legal expertise in what we needed and who could also facilitate the discussion. In the local government department I described earlier, the team there had organized their own appraisal training sessions and had brought in a consultant who responded to their specific requests.

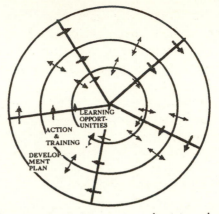

Figure 6.6 *Learning opportunities – action and training – development plan*

The team can also negotiate with other teams for an exchange of skills and knowledge. People can share their expertise with each other, or invite them to try out the machine they operate, or run the computer, or do the next staff briefing.

Team leaders at every level, including the managing director with his or her team of senior managers, need to encourage that kind of sharing to take place. The approach is not based on the 'soft' side of management so scorned by many and that appears to be based on altruism. Businesses are not charities or community centres. Even charities and community centres need to be hard-headed about the way they manage their affairs. The approach is based on sound management sense with a strong economic argument. When people are encouraged to develop their own skills and to pass on the skills they have to others within the team and organization, there are likely to be a number of positive outcomes. Morale improves and as a result disaffection and stress are lowered, with a consequent reduction in lost working days. Quality improves and productivity increases. Staff turnover is reduced. A good balance of both support and challenge maintained within the team ensures the kind of good working relationships and environment needed for those positive outcomes to be achieved.

Part of the challenge is that any action and training undertaken by team members is reviewed and evaluated within the team. Learning is reinforced, ideas and good practices are shared. When one of the members of our team gained new knowledge and skills in dealing with the media, he passed it on to the rest of us. The two people who learnt about the art of putting on successful conferences ran a mini-workshop, not only for this project team but for the others in the organization as well.

The results of the activity and the training are fed back into the team itself through the team review and into the organization's development plan process.

The organization – development plan

The organization will have a business plan. This is part of a wider development plan which must also include the concepts and the practicalities of human resource development (HRD). What I have tried to illustrate here is a process for HRD, using a portfolio approach, that links individual, team and organization development processes in one model.

This part of the development plan attempts to answer the question 'how can we provide the learning structure?' in order to achieve the sort of aims that the organization has set itself.

The organization has carried out its needs analysis on an ongoing basis. It now receives from the team managers the results of the training and action learning programmes that are being carried out. It may often be the case that the organization can benefit from something new that has been learnt and carried out in the workplace and can put it into its development plan. Once our team had learnt about conferences and dealing with the media, an eventual outcome was that the organization set up and ran training courses and consultancy for others in working with the media and putting on conferences. This meant that resources were put into setting up those programmes and supporting the staff who would be acting as trainers and consultants on those issues. The programmes proved highly successful and repaid the investment handsomely.

For an organization wishing to use the portfolio approach, the development plan can be based on the model offered here. The precise way in which it will work through the model must reflect the type, size and style of the organization. Careful preparation, commitment from the top and adequate time given to seeing the process through are the three important ingredients for a successful outcome.

Chapter 7

Some Pitfalls and How to Overcome Them

Introducing this approach and making it successful is not easy. If it were it would probably have been used by most organizations by now. But it is unlikely that something that has as many potential benefits is going to be simple. Some of the pitfalls that may come your way have already been looked at in the previous chapters. In this chapter, I will examine them in a bit more detail and suggest how you might deal with them. The section headings are all the kinds of quotes that I have confronted in the course of helping others to develop a portfolio approach.

'It takes too long'

This comment often arises once managers and trainers realize that this isn't a short cut to training but takes a considerable amount of preparation to put into place. This is largely due to the time it takes to carry out the following four main tasks:

- defining the competences and standards required;
- training in the mentoring and team facilitation skills needed;
- individual portfolio work and the assessment process; and
- setting up and running the team meetings.

We can look at each of those and see how to overcome the arguments.

Defining the competences and standards required

Most of the initial portfolio development work undertaken was done in the absence of recognized sets of standards. These are now widely available. Even where no NVQ standards of competence have been defined as yet, the framework is there for anyone to use.

Training in the mentoring, coaching and team facilitation skills needed

While those skills are needed to run a successful portfolio process, they are needed to manage any well-run organization. The portfolio approach encourages managers to take on and use those skills. Short cuts are not advisable. While there are no doubt a good number of managers and others who already have those skills and can demonstrate them amply, there will be others who cannot. They are the ones who will need to gain those skills, otherwise the process will be a patchy one.

The argument must be that these skills are needed anyway. If it takes six months to develop them throughout the organization, it will be time well spent even if nothing else happened. Part of the strategy of introducing a portfolio approach might be to ensure that managers are equipped with those skills, which are all about empowering and developing staff.

In one engineering company where I helped to develop the approach, they insisted on starting with first line managers. The aim was to help them to develop their own portfolios and hence their competences, and to act as mentors and team facilitators with their own staff. The assumption that the organization made was that middle managers already had the necessary skills to pick up the process. This was not the case. When the first line managers introduced the idea of portfolio development, their own managers failed to support them, lacking the understanding and the skills needed to work with their own staff teams. The senior managers, concerned that the investment they had made was about to be sabotaged, set about ensuring that middle management had the competences to empower and develop their staff.

Individual portfolio work and the assessment process

It takes time for an individual to develop a portfolio. Moreover, it takes the time of others too: the mentor, other colleagues, supervisors and managers, and the assessor. For a person to start a portfolio of prior experience and learning from scratch in order to gain accreditation in a set of standards and competences, it may take anything up to a year or two. Even the kind of portfolio that asks only that an individual jots down some current experience or observation, takes up some time in the week that might be used for other, presumably productive, work.

The argument is that, in the former case, gaining a qualification through more traditional routes takes about the same time anyway, and often includes having to study for skills unnecessarily. In the latter case, it is a fallacy that people are always engaged in productive work. Much of their time is probably spent on putting things right or at least in replicating tasks inappropriately simply because nobody ever stopped to reflect on what was going on.

Probably the most effective strategy is to persuade the person questioning the process to try it out with your help. That is why, at the beginning of this book, I asked you to try the process out for yourself. It is likely that if you have got this far, you were either convinced already or found it a useful experience.

Setting up and running the process, including team meetings

Setting up any process takes time. How long depends on what is going on in the organization at the time. Where there are regular team meetings, where communication is good between departments and hierarchies, where individuals have an opportunity to discuss their progress and their concerns with their manager and each other, there will be little more to put into place. Where few or none of these things occur now, it will take longer.

Where that kind of learning and development environment is not in place, it is worth taking anything up to a year to prepare the ground. Where such conditions prevail there may be a reluctance among senior managers to make time for change. There are two scenarios. The first will be where managers have already alerted themselves to the need for change and are seeking ways of going about it. In that case, preparation for a portfolio approach as part of your development plan can be the way forward. The second is where you are attempting to introduce change to a cynical management. The strategy here must include providing the evidence of a need for change and the expected outcomes of investing and not investing the time.

'It's expensive'

If it takes time, it will cost money. It may mean engaging an outside consultant to assist in the process. There are some tangible costs: the engagement of an outside consultant and trainers if needed, and the cost of producing portfolio folders and accompanying material if desired. There are also many hidden costs: team meetings, individual time taken in developing portfolios, mentoring time and so on.

Against all this must be the presentation of a clear set of costed targets of the expected outcomes over a given realistic period. Part of the preparation to be done before going to anyone else with the notion of portfolio development in an organization, is to make out a rough cost–benefit analysis. There will undoubtedly be benefits related to the qualitative aspects of people's work and conditions: their morale, self-confidence, etc. Benefits must also be presented in clear quantitative terms: current and expected productivity, staff turnover and expected reduction in cost. In the end, it is a better profit and loss account that will determine the extent to which there is management support for any process.

'It's complicated'

One of the mistakes I made when presenting the concept to the managers in one organization was to begin by showing them the model for portfolio development. It may have been fine for trainers or others who were quite enthusiastic about models, but it wasn't for them at that stage. It was too complicated and seemed to bear little relationship to their own needs.

In fact, the essence of the approach is very simple and needs to be presented very simply without being patronizing. It is a way of individuals, teams and the organization as a whole learning to improve performance. People will be asked to record what they have done and to discuss this with their colleagues and their managers. A strategy for this will be developed and there will be a need for some preparatory work – for example, in defining our objectives and the competences we require, and in training for some managers in the skills needed.

The results will be:

1. Individuals who can provide evidence of their competence. This will go into a personal portfolio and help them to gain accreditation to NVQ standards or others required.
2. Teams who are more aware of their own strengths and what is required of them; together with an action programme to become more skilled.
3. An organization with fully competent managers and staff, ready and able to improve performances continually.

'It doesn't mean us'

Most training and organization development work requested by managers leaves the higher echelons unscathed. I have heard many senior managers say 'yes that's just what our people need' as though it has nothing to do with them. One of the refreshing changes that it is good to observe is when senior management teams do commit not only the resources to make the process work, but their own time to ensure that it works.

One of the stipulations is that the process does start at the top of the hierarchy and continues to involve senior management. When the process is seen and experienced as an integral part of managing and developing, it will be working successfully; and that can only happen with the full active participation of senior managers, office juniors and everyone in between.

'We've tried all these things before'

The chances are fairly high that any organization looking at taking up this approach will already have tried things before. Some no doubt worked. Others may have fallen by the wayside, leaving the cynics (probably the ones who sabotaged the process in the first place) to decry anything that smacks of yet another 'project' or 'method'. Dealing with those critics is not easy.

The tactic is first of all to emphasize that this is not a project but a way of managing better, and that it will be put into practice with specific work-related targets. The second tactic is to engage those who view the proposal in a negative light in trying it out for themselves.

'Why do I need to put things into a portfolio?'

This may be a question asked by an individual staff member who has been asked to record things by his or her manager. The question is as often born out of suspicion – 'what do they want to do with it; are they asking me to spy on my mates?' – as it is out of anxiety – 'what am I supposed to write down? I've not written anything since I left school 16 years ago and I couldn't do it very well then'.

This is where the briefing sessions for staff at all levels must be carefully and sensitively handled. Stress that the recordings and the portfolios are people's personal property. Individuals may show what they have recorded or they may keep certain parts to themselves. The essential point to make is that everyone has something to learn and everyone has something to offer. What is far more important than how something is recorded is what can be learnt from the experience that is recorded.

'It's not what managers are supposed to do'

There may be varied opinions about what managers are supposed to do. If nothing else, a comment like this can lead to a very fruitful debate and to different understanding and practice. I used to run training courses where the first question was 'what are managers supposed to do?'. This invariably led to the programme for the whole course being defined by the participants in quite a different way from what most of them had expected.

The most effective way of tackling this comment is to return it as a question. Managers who see their role in the more directive and autocratic mould, having little faith in the ability and trustworthiness of their staff, will find it harder to come to terms with the style more often demanded of the portfolio approach than the leader who believes in enabling and empowering staff to achieve agreed targets. Managers who carry out a role more akin to reactive administrators than to positive developers will have a harder job taking on this approach.

There is little question that the portfolio approach is demanding of managers and requires them to have a range of competences themselves. The following are some of them.

Conceptual skills

Managers will need to have a clear understanding of the relationship between what an individual might put into a portfolio and the potential for change within the organization. This means that the manager should have a clear grasp of the whole concept of the portfolio approach and an ability to put theory into practice.

Listening skills

Perhaps the key skill needed for this approach is active listening. This is a skill that is much talked about and seldom as developed as individuals believe it is. It can be a very powerful tool for anyone and is the basis of most of the skills that follow.

Facilitation skills

Literally making something easier. The essence of good facilitation skills is to enable people to arrive at their own conclusions about what they should do and how they could best do it. In other words, it is an empowering tool, encouraging others to take more responsibility for themselves and their work. The manager who does that not only has a responsible and effective work team, he or she also has more time to take on the management tasks of planning and developing new ideas. In the portfolio approach, facilitation skills are crucial both in working with an individual portfolio-builder and with the team.

Teamwork skills

If the manager did not have them before, he or she would need to develop teamwork skills for this approach. The team review demands that the team leader draws out members of the group, keeps others from dominating it, is able to keep the group to its task and the process, and is able to summarize and help the group arrive at conclusions and action.

Those competences seldom come naturally. Often managers fail to have them because they have no positive model from which to draw and no tuition. It is unrealistic to expect managers to work effectively with their teams just because they are managers. The preparation for putting a portfolio approach into practice ensures that managers have those skills.

Questioning skills

Along with listening, the ability to ask the relevant question in the appropriate way is an underused yet important skill. Questioning skills are valuable in interviewing, project management, appraisals, tendering and monitoring – to name a few management tasks that are not even part of this discussion.

Mentoring skills

This may be an entirely new role requested of managers; in fact it may be a role expected of staff at all levels and is therefore a potential introduction to management. Since the mentor may be someone from another department, not having any direct management function, the mentor role is one that all managers are likely to need. The mentor is a vital part of the jigsaw within the portfolio approach. This means that training for people to act as mentors is a central part of the preparation. The likely implication of simply moving into this role is one of heightened morale and feeling of involvement.

Coaching skills

Coaching is sometimes seen as a whole approach to management. It is certainly a valuable part of the portfolio approach and falls precisely within the management style needed. It is particularly relevant where the staff member has identified, through his or her portfolio, a competence that needs to be developed. More often than not this will mean that something can be learnt in the work environment. The manager's job may well be to provide some coaching to help the member of staff to demonstrate required standards of competence. Coaching may be part of the organization's culture, or it may not. If not, it will have to become so for the portfolio approach to be developed.

Communication skills

The manager must be able to talk with people at all levels of ability and authority. The portfolio approach demands that people talk to each other across the organization in all directions on equal terms. The fact that some people are responsible for deciding on the overall direction of the entire organization and others are responsible for making a machine work properly, does not mean that they cannot and should not talk with each other, since each affects the other in some way.

Negotiation skills

Connected with communication is the ability to negotiate. Assertiveness is a part of that competence. The manager will be expected to decide upon and bring to his or her own manager and own team the key issues that need to be raised. There will be other, sometimes competing, requests for action. This may prove discomforting for some, but can be an enlivening and healthy process as long as people understand it and have the negotiating skills.

All the above skills are required for the portfolio process. If they all exist now and are used to the fullest extent, it will be easy to put into practice the portfolio approach. If they do not all exist, setting up a portfolio process will be the catalyst for putting them into place.

'What difference is it going to make?'

A final question that may be posed is whether or not it will make any real difference in the long run. It is a question that nobody can answer with any degree of certainty. There are too many cases of 'it depends on. . .'. Most of what it depends on has been explored here. What can be said with confidence is that if all the preparation and the procedures are put into place as described in this book a great deal will happen to change things for the better.

Chapter 8

Accreditation or Effectiveness?

There are differing views as to whether the purpose of building a portfolio is to gain accreditation in the desired vocation or whether it is to demonstrate and improve one's personal and professional effectiveness. It is of course a spurious argument as the two are inextricably entwined. There is, however, a problem to address before making too many assumptions about the relationship between the two.

The development of portfolios for personal and professional effectiveness may lead, if desired, to accreditation. The real question is whether accreditation is necessarily an indicator of effectiveness. That is what I want to explore in this chapter.

The relationship between NVQs and the portfolio approach

As part of the whole training revolution, NVQs are designed so that people can build up a range of units, through work-based experience and training programmes from a variety of sources, towards a National Record of Vocational Achievement (NROVA). The procedure is designed to be flexible in terms of time and selected units of competence.

Portfolios can be developed to provide the evidence of competence, which is then assessed. Where the evidence is deemed sufficient, credit is given. In this way, qualifications become based more on practical application of competence at work than on an ability to pass tests and study for examinations. The intention is that accreditation will indeed be a marker for competence. A growing number of people who have been through the process are a testimony to that fact.

The difficulty comes in the translation of intention into practice. The NVQ system is not intended to be a training or a learning programme. It is a method of assessing performance against clearly defined criteria.

That has not stopped organizations from attempting to use the standards of competence as a guideline for training courses. One major government department is even embarking on a major training programme based on the standards of competence for MCI, apparently ignoring the fact that most of their managers will already be able to demonstrate abilities in many of those required.

It is vital to get the idea across within your own organization that NVQs and the MCI are not items for a training agenda and that helping people to develop their portfolios is a more productive route to the achievement of excellence.

At the very least a portfolio is a record of an individual's prior learning. My theme, however, is that it forms the basis of a complete development process, of which part of the equation is the setting of standards. NVQs have pioneered the way for the setting of those standards in a clear, concise and precise way. The lead bodies from the various industries and professions have already done most of the necessary and time-consuming work. It is now up to the organization to adopt and adapt as appropriate and for the individual to select what he or she can offer as evidence in order to gain accreditation.

The relevance of competences

The range of skills, knowledge and understanding applied to a particular activity or area of work has been put together in the generic word 'competences'. A competent skipper of a sailing vessel will not only have the skills to make sure that the rigging is correctly set and can manoeuvre the boat, but will have knowledge about wind direction, tides and currents, and an understanding of the nature of the elements and how the boat will react in certain conditions. He or she will also need to be able to handle a crew, organize equipment, monitor maintenance procedures, know about safety precautions and be able to handle emergency situations. There will be a need for decisive action where appropriate and an ability to react quickly and flexibly with a clear knowledge of what is feasible.

Many of those competences are transferable to other situations. The question is: what are the competences needed for a person to carry out a particular task or job? Some may be specific only to that job. The sailor, for example, may have gained competences in managing a crew and organizing equipment in another, unrelated area of activity. It is less likely that he or she would have learnt how to steer a boat or set the rigging without actually being aboard the vessel.

Every general area of work can be sub-divided into discrete jobs which can then be sub-divided into smaller tasks. Each of those work areas, jobs and tasks can then be examined in terms of the competences required to carry them out. The competences may then be translated into the performance indicators that will show the standard and level to which any competence is performed. This scientific approach is the one adopted through the NVQ process.

The individual

For an individual building a portfolio in order to gain accreditation, the standards of competence laid down are the ones he or she will have to demonstrate. What is important is the process that the person goes through in order to arrive at the stage of accreditation. With set standards there may be a temptation to follow the requirements as though they are a set of instructions.

The mentor needs to take the candidate through the competence statements and get him or her to think about them in relation to the actual job. There is often a need to make a conceptual jump from what is on the paper and what it means in practice. For example, in the MCI's Occupational Standards for Managers, Level I, one of the four key roles is to:

- 'manage operations'.

Within this there is a unit labelled:

- 'maintain and improve service and product operations'.

Under that unit there are two elements, one of which is:

- 'create and maintain the necessary conditions for productive work',

and under that heading there are eight performance indicators, one of which is:

- 'a sufficient supply of resources of the necessary quality is established and maintained to meet customer requirements'.

This seems to be a relevant requirement of any manager. When initially presented to a group of first line managers, their expressions were somewhat blank. Because the standards relate to any manager managing anything, the words must be made to mean something. The first task is to examine what the statements mean in relation to the person's own specific work context.

Questions in this instance seem to be:

- who is the customer and how can I find out their requirements?
- what resources are needed?
- what is a sufficient supply?
- how can I assess the quality?
- what systems are in place to maintain a supply of resources?
- what can I do to make sure I have the answers to these questions?

When the managers were asked and then answered these questions for themselves, the requirement began to make sense and became relevant to them. In some cases they could very quickly demonstrate that they did what was required now. Others were unsure whether or not they could really show that they carried out this function adequately. A few were certain that they had never done it, but recognized that it was something that they should be doing.

It was through the process of question and answer, and through the managers examining their own experience and recording this in their portfolios, that they understood the relevance of the competence requirements.

When an individual is developing a portfolio for personal development, part of the process is to help that person identify the competences desired. That may be helped by the standards already set. The acceptance of personal responsibility of taking that further step of deciding for oneself the competences one needs is a healthy move. Because this is even more difficult than redefining set standards, the assistance of a mentor is crucial in this process. The mentor can be another learner. Two people can very productively assist each other, using the kind of procedures described in Chapter 2.

The team

Working within a team, the standards set through NVQs become an even more potent tool for development. Competence requirements come from two main sources. One is the awarding body, which may be an industry's single body or a consortium set up to award NVQs. Any body that awards an NVQ will be approved by the National Council for Vocational Qualifications (NCVQ). The second source will be the team itself.

It is inside the team that the most immediate information lies as to what competences are needed. The relevance of the external standards must be tested against those needs. Teams who take a close look at the standards of competence required for their type and level of operation will find them of enormous benefit once they ask the right questions. The sterile way will be for a group of people to go through the standards, checking them off as they do so and ignoring the ones that do not seem to be relevant.

The organization

A few large organizations are synonymous with the lead bodies that represent them, like British Rail, British Gas and the Post Office. Most are represented by a consortium of people from the appropriate industry. In any event, the organization must set its own targets before deciding upon the relevance of the set standards.

The setting of occupational standards has been a real breakthrough in the drive towards quality and excellence. But before complacency sets in, it is as well to remind organizations that it is they who should be taking the lead for their own development. I know of managers, including training managers, in several organizations who have taken wholesale the standards of competence without examining them for their relevance to their own requirements.

Much work has gone into ensuring that standards are complete and precise. This does not mean that organizations need do nothing. They must ensure that the standards and the statements of competence really say what they need to say to make them relevant. In other words, they may have to do some interpreting before asking their staff to satisfy the requirements.

How portfolios relate to accreditation requirements

Individuals have to provide evidence to receive credit through the NVQ system. The portfolios they produce must therefore reflect the accreditation requirements. How the portfolio does that is up to the individual.

Some competences are straightforward to demonstrate. Where, for example, a particular skill in a manufacturing process is called for, the demonstration is the tangible object produced to the required standard. The portfolio at the very least can show a photograph of the finished object, or a letter or certificate proving that the article has been made by the candidate and is of the required standard. Such a letter can be from the supervisor or manager, or a satisfied customer.

Other competences are less easy to prove, which is where a degree of flexibility and creativity is normally needed. Statements of competence requirements include performance criteria and range indicators – jargon for the precise standards expected and the kinds of things that can be shown. Being precise about imprecise disciplines is naturally enough a problem for the designers of standards. The solution lies in the hands of the people who present their portfolios.

Managers and trainers must be aware of the difficulty faced by many people when they are asked to provide tangible evidence of intangible skills. How does one demonstrate an ability to 'establish and maintain the trust and support of one's subordinates' for example? (MCI Level I) On one level, it is possible to show the processes that someone has gone through to try and gain trust and support. It is harder to provide real proof that this has been successful or of what could be changed. The portfolio-builder may need help to look beyond some of the more superficial aspects of the task to see how to demonstrate the development of trust.

One of the ways that candidates for an NVQ can most fruitfully build a portfolio of evidence is by focusing on a particular project at work that will entail using a whole range of the required competences. This may be a project undertaken in the past or one that is specifically set up with an NVQ in mind. It should be real and relevant to the work of the individual and the organization, rather than being constructed as a kind of 'exam piece'.

There is a tension between such work being 'competence-led' or 'learner led'. The competence statements are an excellent guide to the kinds of things that someone needs to know or be able to do. They can be counterproductive if used only to gain a credit. In the effort to reach high standards of competence, we must not forget what it is all about: the improvement in the quality of goods and services being delivered to the customer, whether that customer is the purchaser of a roll of wallpaper, a disabled person receiving care in the community or a manager in another department needing information from you.

Developing a portfolio from experience and demonstrating competence related to accreditation requirements is, in my view, a process more compatible with real individual and work needs that starting with a list of competences and working to them.

Organizations are increasingly expected to conform to British and European standards of quality. They too need to develop portfolios to demonstrate their readiness and fitness to receive the approval of the awarding body. Firms who work towards the achievement of BS5750 or ISO9000, or schemes like Investors in People, are conscious of the need to show both to their own staff and to the outside world their commitment to quality. A great deal of energy and thought goes into achieving the requirements; and not an inconsiderable cost investment in receiving recognition and maintaining it.

If the organization engages in a portfolio-building process for itself, it will be in a strong position to demonstrate its effectiveness to any awarding body. More important than that, it will be able to use the portfolio to demonstrate its standards of quality to its customers, its staff and its investors.

Portfolio assessment

A number of different people may be involved in the assessment procedure. The first and most crucial person is the portfolio-builder. There may also be colleagues, a mentor or adviser, a manager or supervisor and an internal or external assessor. The organization itself may be a part of the assessment where it has established a system for portfolio development.

Whoever is carrying out an assessment, there are five basic principles by which evidence is measured. These are:

- validity;
- reliability;
- sufficiency;
- authenticity; and
- currency.

These principles are described in Susan Simosko's book *APL: A Practical Guide for Professionals* (Kogan Page). I will look at them here only in terms of the questions that need to be asked in each case.

Validity

Does what is being demonstrated match what is being assessed? Is it a real measure of the person's competence in relation to the standard required? Is it relevant to what is sought? How well does the evidence match the performance criteria?

Reliability

How do the assessors' views match up with each other? Is there sufficient agreement among all the relevant parties to assure

reliability? Do the assessors have a clear and consistent understanding of what is required of the candidate and of the assessment
process itself?

Sufficiency

Is there enough evidence of different kinds to indicate that the
competence standards have been achieved? Have the assessors
themselves been given a clear guideline about the amount that is
likely to be too much or too little to be of benefit? Has this information been passed on to the candidate?

Authenticity

How does the portfolio clearly demonstrate that it is a true reflection of the candidate's own competence? Is the evidence an
affirmed representation of what the candidate has done? How can
you tell that the claims made in the portfolio are authentic?

Currency

How well does the portfolio evidence reflect the current competence of the candidate? Where evidence from past experience is
given, how has the person shown the present circumstances in
which the competence is used?

The above five guiding principles and the related questions are
useful for any of the parties in the portfolio development process
to keep in mind. The issue of assessment is a thorny one in any
circumstance. In most cases assessors are distant, even unknown,
to the candidate whose career may depend upon their judgement.
In the portfolio process, the wider the assessment and the closer
the assessors to the portfolio owner the better. The aim is for portfolio assessment to have been a process of consultation before it
even arrives on the desk of a person formally appointed to recommend accreditation to the awarding body.

The people who may be involved in that consulting assessment
process are the five groupings I mentioned at the beginning of this
section.

Self

Part of the discipline learnt through using portfolios is that of assessment. The very act of recording experience in an ordered way and reflecting on what has been learnt is a self-assessment process. Once a portfolio has been developed to the stage where it provides evidence of specifically required competences, the individual goes through another stage of assessment.

For this the person, alone or more probably with the support of someone else, can use the principles for measuring evidence and apply them to what he or she has produced so far. The more rigorous someone is able to be in making a considered analysis of the evidence, the better that person will be in applying that ability in everyday work. This aspect of assessment is to be encouraged right from the start of the process and as an integral part of it.

Peer

An extension of the self-assessment process is the assistance that can be given by colleagues engaged in their own portfolio development. Two or three people working in a disciplined way can be a most effective way of giving and getting feedback. They will be helped by applying the five principles and asking the questions of each other. People may well need some guidance and practice in asking the appropriate questions and giving responses. Developing the ability to be open honest and direct without being judgemental when giving feedback is not easy, especially when this has not been a cultural norm within the organization.

Expertise of this kind can be developed within the team. The team leader can provide the tuition, or this can be the task of a tutor brought in specifically to assist in the process.

Mentor

The mentor, or adviser, needs skills in being able to take the portfolio owner through the assessment procedure. The mentor must be fully aware of the criteria of the awarding body, the competences and standards being sought, and the principles guiding the assessment process.

It will be the task of the mentor to take the candidate through the questions that he or she needs to be asking and to ensure that all the key points have been addressed. The mentor should be able to offer the objective advice that will enable the candidate to decide when to submit his or her portfolio for formal assessment.

Manager

The manager or supervisor of the portfolio-builder has an important role to play in assisting in the assessment procedure. Since much of the evidence contained within the portfolio is likely to come from performance in the workplace, the manager will be in a position to observe directly the 'raw material' for that evidence. Such direct evidence is an invaluable source for the demonstration of competence.

The manager can assist by observing, by giving immediate feedback, by offering supportive evidence, by recording what has been achieved by the candidate and by offering opportunities for further practice in the workplace. The manager is the key person in enabling peer assessment through the team, or in encouraging more informal peer assessment sessions.

Assessor

The assessor may be appointed and trained internally within an organization or be an external assessor approved by the awarding body. In some cases there may a number of assessors making individual judgements or meeting as a panel. Whoever the assessor and whatever the circumstance there are some common points that must be observed for the assessment to be seen as a positive part of a continuing process.

The first thing to bear in mind is that the portfolio process, linked to national standards or not, is intended as a very different experience from other routes to accreditation. Most other routes depend on somebody being judged by someone else as to whether they have passed or failed. Quite often the dividing line is narrow and sometimes spurious. On occasions a failure will mean setting someone back a year or more in terms of their career development.

The assessment of a portfolio is different. There are still criteria and principles to be met. People, however, do not pass or fail. They do, or they do not yet, provide the evidence of competences against a set of standards. The difference may appear slight, but it is an important and subtle difference that needs to be communicated to the candidate. The candidate might personally present the portfolio to an assessor. In other cases, the assessor may not actually meet the candidate. Whichever the situation, the portfolio should stand on its own, and be capable of being understood and assessed without additional explanation. If the assessor has to ask many questions for clarification, it is likely that the candidate needs to make things clearer within the portfolio.

Part of the assessor's job is to provide comments and questions that will be helpful to the candidate's continuing development. Where a candidate has not provided adequate evidence, the assessor should point out where this is the case and make comments to assist the candidate in knowing what he or she needs to do to fill in the gaps. Where a candidate's portfolio has fulfilled all the requirements, the assessor can still point to areas that help the candidate to consider what the next steps are in his or her development, based on the level following the one assessed.

Finally, the assessor should reinforce the notion that portfolio development is a continual process and avoid the message that the portfolio is now complete. The assessment, and the assessor, need to be seen as a part of the process and not the end of it. Accreditation is an acknowledgement and a celebration of a stage of development.

I remember well my relief at escaping school. I never wanted to study again as school had not been a positive experience. Fortunately I overcame my own negativity by discovering totally different ways of learning. I remember later the satisfaction at gaining a degree after six years' part-time study through the Open University. This was, although hard, a positive experience and it encouraged my enthusiasm for continuing the learning process, partly helped by the process of continuous assessment both by myself and by my tutors. It was given a knock only by the need to take examinations and await the result of an anonymous assessment based on a few hours' writing. This was, it seemed, an inevitability and I accepted it as such. On reflection, it added nothing to my own ability other than the capacity to work in examination conditions, something that I have not needed to do in any other circumstance. What I have had to do is to respond to questions or requests verbally and, in my own time, in writing. Doing that to get my degree would have been a better preparation for me.

The portfolio assessment process should as far as possible reflect and contribute to the whole portfolio approach. The assessors need to have a good appreciation of the concepts behind portfolio development and be sensitive to individual and organizational needs as well as the requirements of awarding bodies. The best way to prepare for the assessment of others is for the assessor to go through the portfolio process personally.

The organization

The organization participates in assessment through having established a learning system that involves portfolio development. Where the system follows the model described earlier, assessment is built in through the team and organization reviews, and the appraisal and the analysis of corporate strengths and human resources. This can all be measured against the goals, the development plan and the required competences.

The basis for the assessment is how far the organization has demonstrated its achievements against its defined objectives of enhanced quality and performance.

Portfolios for effectiveness

This chapter heading asks whether portfolio development is for accreditation or greater personal and professional effectiveness.

My response has been that it has to be about both, but there must be a cautiousness attached to both the question and the response. If the aim is greater effectiveness, then accreditation can be a route towards that; it is certainly a tangible recognition of that effectiveness. Greater effectiveness, however, is brought about through the process of portfolio development, not by the gaining of the accreditation when that portfolio is presented.

If the main aim is accreditation there is no guarantee that greater effectiveness will be the result, although the chances are high that something will have happened. The real concern must be that accreditation and qualification for their own sake will not lead to the desired long-term aim of improving quality. In Chapter 1, I defined the following attributes as those that will be most sought after:

- flexibility;
- self-motivation;
- communication skills; and
- a willingness and ability to develop new skills.

People who are effective in those areas will be able to use whatever other talents they have to the best of their ability. They are attributes that will turn a shop assistant into an accomplished sales person, a manager into a leader and an unemployed plumber into a successful business person. Effectiveness is what counts. The proof of that effectiveness lies in the new accreditation system. Getting there through portfolio development will bring the two things together. All we have to do is to be true to the process.

Chapter 9

Setting up a Portfolio Approach

By now you will have thought a lot about the portfolio approach: the concepts behind it, its practicalities, its advantages and disadvantages, and how you might be able to apply it within your own work. You may still have some questions. Those questions may not be answered until you have tried the process out in practice individually and with the organization.

In this chapter I will look at how you need to prepare the ground for a portfolio approach within your organization. Most of this will have been dealt with previously, so it is laid out here in the form of a series of exercises for you to use. You will need a notepad by you for this work, or it may be used as a team exercise with the responses written on a flipchart or board.

Establishing the aims and setting targets

- Write down your aims in developing a portfolio approach:
    1. for the organization
    2. for teams within the organization
    3. for individuals within the organization
    4. for customers of the organization

- Write down the targets, both quantitative and qualitative, that you want to achieve in the first three/six/twelve months of operation of a portfolio approach:

1. for the organization
2. for teams
3. for individuals
4. for customers

Selling it throughout the organization

- Write down what you are going to say to sell the idea:

  1. to the director/s and other senior managers
  2. to middle management/team leaders
  3. to all other staff
  4. to customers

- Write down how you are going to present your case:

  1. to senior management
  2. to middle management
  3. to other staff
  4. to customers

Involving people at all levels

- Write down who you can involve from the start of the process, giving consideration to as wide a cross-section as feasible.

- Give at least three examples of how you can involve those people, noting the advantages and disadvantages of each way.

Agreeing the standards and competences

- Write down the resources you have or can get to assist you in the development of competence statements.

- Write down the methods you will use to gain the support and agreement of others within the organization that the standards and competences are the ones required.

Using current systems

- Write down what systems, meetings etc the organization already has that will ease the setting up and maintenance of a portfolio approach.

- Write down how you will go about incorporating a portfolio approach into current systems.

- Write down any additional systems that will need to be developed.

Making it relevant

- Check back through your responses so far; then write down how you will illustrate the relevance of the portfolio approach to the needs of:

  1. senior managers
  2. middle managers
  3. other staff
  4. customers

Preparing and training key staff

- Give consideration to the human resources of the organization. Write down who (individuals or functions) will best fulfil the roles of:

  1. mentors/advisers
  2. supervisors/tutors
  3. team leaders/facilitators
  4. assessors

- Looking back at the people you have described or named, write down the skills that you believe they will need, how you can find out whether or not they have them, and the preparation and training that you can arrange for them.

Deciding on your development plan

- Now write down your plan for setting up a portfolio approach in your organization.

- What will help this to work?

- What may prevent it from working?

- How will you overcome any potential difficulties?

A pilot scheme

- In the case of your wishing to test the approach out first in part of the organization, write down where you will start, giving at least three examples in order of preference.

- Write down your plan and a realistic timetable for the pilot scheme.

Resources and costs

- Make a note of what material, information and other resources you propose to supply, and to whom.

- Bearing in mind costs of current processes and systems within the organization, what is your best estimate of the additional costs of developing and installing a portfolio approach, to include staff time, material, training and consultancy fees?

Monitoring and evaluation

- In either the pilot scheme or the full programme, write down what procedures you will propose for continual monitoring and a regular evaluation of the process against the targets set.

Summary

- Finally, for your own portfolio:

  1. Write down what you have learnt from your work on these exercises.
  2. Take the action that you have decided upon; then provide evidence to demonstrate what you have done and learnt.
  3. Note from this what competences you feel you need to develop further.
  4. Decide how you can best enhance those competences and take the opportunity to do so.
  5. Summarize your experience in going through this process.

Chapter 10

Organizing a Portfolio

Whatever the purpose of the portfolio, and notwithstanding that it should be as flexible as possible, it needs to be organized from the start or it will turn out to be a collection of material that only the compiler will understand. If the portfolio-builder then wants to show it to anyone else, in particular an assessor, a great deal of extra time and work will have to go into putting it into some sort of order.

One of the first 'portfolios' I saw was a pile of papers, photographs and objects crammed into a cardboard box. The compiler went through this material, presenting it to a group engaged in learning about portfolios. Each item she drew out of the box illustrated a significant experience and competence she had developed over the past few years. She had obviously gained a great deal of self-knowledge and self-confidence in compiling the material and it left her audience enraptured. But she could hardly have put the box down on the floor and expected the rest of us to make any sense out of it. The owner of the box and its contents was a training manager with the Girl Guides Association (the largest youth organization in Britain) and this was in 1985. As the concepts and practicalities of portfolio development became clearer, she saw the contents as the raw material from which she could develop her portfolio. She later became instrumental in introducing the portfolio approach within the Girl Guides movement.

In this chapter, I will offer some guidelines on the organizing of portfolios. The purpose of the portfolio is for personal, professional, team or organization development, and ideally for all four. Since the process for portfolio-building is rather different in each case, I will deal with them separately, using the same cycles of portfolio development from the models already described.

Personal development

Before compiling material for the portfolio, it is as well to consider the following points:

- Something will be needed to contain the information and evidence; probably a ring binder, with a wallet for additional material (photos etc).
- The more flexible the container or binder, the easier it will be to add to the material, or to take things out or change the order; important if the portfolio is later to be used for professional development as a route to accreditation.
- A cover page with basic information is essential. Such information should include name of compiler, purpose of portfolio, date/s, address, location of work or place of study as appropriate, contact names and functions of others involved (mentor, manager, colleagues etc).

1(a) Describing experience: the index

This will be at the front of the portfolio and will be added to regularly. It will also need to be organized flexibly.

The index is the brief description, or 'chapter headings', of the experiences described within the portfolio. Each item in the index will need to be referenced with the relevant page number (hence the need for flexibility). It may be that the individual decides not to go any further with the description of a particular item from the index. In that case it will probably be useful for the item to remain indexed with no page number for potential later use.

1(b) Describing experience: the story

The story of each experience is summarized. Even where the compiler has little intention of showing the portfolio to anyone else, it is as well to get into the habit of recording the story in a concise and clear way with no technical jargon, so that it can be read and understood by somebody outside the situation.

The compiler decides whether or not the experience described is one that he or she wants to share with anyone else, or whether it is to be kept confidential.

2. Identifying learning from experience: the discovery

There is a choice now. The compiler can either continue to record the next stage directly after the experience, simply putting a new heading 'what I discovered', or can collate all the discoveries and put them into a separate section. If the latter course is taken, there will have to be a cross-referencing system so that claims of what has been learnt are traceable to specific events or personal experiences of the compiler.

3. The demonstration of practice: the proof

Giving proof that what the compiler claims to have learnt is actually being carried out in practice, should be no less rigorous because the purpose is personal development than it would be for professional accreditation. The greater the discipline, the higher the personal satisfaction is likely to be.

The same principles should be applied here as for the assessment process: the evidence should be valid, reliable, sufficient, authentic and current. The proof should also be drawn from a variety of sources using different kinds of material.

The compiler can add the proof to each section of experience, or put it into a separate section. The latter may be preferable. What is important is that any evidence can be extracted from the portfolio or moved in order to show it as the compiler desires at a later stage. The proof must be cross-referenced with the experience and the learning claims.

4. Establishing learning needs: ownership

The portfolio now moves into the stage that acknowledges it as a continuing developmental process rather than one intended to be definitive. The compiler should summarize the main things that he or she wishes to develop as a new or an improved competence. There is the same choice of where to put this section, as long as there is consistency and the appropriate system of cross-referencing as necessary.

5(a) Identifying and taking up learning opportunities: growth

The portfolio reflects the compiler's learning contract. This should include:

- the competence to be developed, or the subject of the learning;
- the ways in which the compiler intends to gain the competence; and
- a timetable for the process.

5(b) Identifying and taking up learning opportunities: review

This is a different kind of demonstration. It is proof that the portfolio compiler has set up his or her own learning experience and has grown in competence as a consequence. The review needs to show not just what happened and how, but what the results were.

Professional development

The essential difference between a portfolio for personal development and one for professional development lies in the requirements laid down by an external body. A personal portfolio may be adapted to show the competences that have been attained; a professional portfolio starts out with those competence requirements in mind.

The organization of a portfolio for professional development gives more emphasis to the level and standards required by the awarding body for the qualification sought. An NVQ credit may be given for individual units up to the entire set of competences required for a full award.

Part of the preparation for the candidate is to know what the full requirements are. The portfolio-builder, with the help of a mentor, should ensure that he or she understands the meaning and relevance of the requirements and includes them within the portfolio, ready for cross-referencing.

The cover page of the portfolio, as well as giving the full name and address of the compiler and names and roles of other people involved, should include a brief resumé of the person's career. Any certificates, diplomas etc relevant to the accreditation for which the portfolio is being submitted should also be noted. The work setting of the candidate should be described, giving information about the type of business, its size, location and structure.

Apart from that, the general structure of this portfolio can follow the same sequence as before, although the content may be focused differently.

1(a) Describing experience: the index

The index is set out as before, with the addition of cross-referencing for the competence requirements sought.

Before submission of the portfolio, the candidate will need to indicate where the requirements are illustrated. Extraneous material should be taken out; a bulky portfolio is not necessarily the best. Where the compiler, with the advice of a mentor, is satisfied that the competences are amply demonstrated by a few of the experiences presented, there is every advantage in only submitting those. The candidate should always go back to the five principles for assessment to check what to leave in and what to take out.

1(b) Describing experience: the story

A summary of the experience should include clear information about the nature of the compiler's involvement. It is the candidate's competence that is to be assessed, not anybody else's except as a consequence of what the candidate may have done.

Wherever possible, the story must provide a concise background to the performance of the compiler, indicating where this can be corroborated. This evidence is the *performance evidence*. Where it is not possible to provide such information, there will have to be *supplementary evidence*. This will be supportive to the candidate's claims of competence.

Where technical terms are used they should be explained. Assessors may have little detailed knowledge of the kind of work that a candidate does and jargon is not appreciated.

2. Identifying learning from experience: the discovery

The candidate will be able to reinforce his or her claim to competence through giving a summary of the main learning points attained. While not every experience will demonstrate competence, it should have been the preparation for development leading to practical action, preferably in the normal course of the person's work.

The ability to identify what has been learnt is an important competence in itself. Assessors should take this into account when responding to a candidate's portfolio.

3. The demonstration of practice: the proof

It is the performance evidence that will be sought. Supplementary evidence may be offered when the former is not feasible – this might include supporting certificates to show the candidate has completed a relevant training programme, or personal statements from the candidate or a manager or colleague. Supplementary evidence may indicate knowledge and conceptual understanding, but not necessarily the ability of the candidate to perform to the required standard. Both are helpful, since one adds weight to the other.

The evidence given must be clearly and carefully cross-referenced to the competence statement or statements to which it relates, indicating the unit, the performance criteria and range indicators. Any referencing system should be explained. It is helpful for the evidence to be given a separate section, again carefully cross-referenced to the relevant story.

4. Establishing learning needs: ownership

Once the candidate has provided proof of having some of the competences required, he or she can decide what has not yet been satisfactorily demonstrated.

This section may or may not be in the final presentation of the portfolio. If it is, it will indicate the development process that the candidate has gone through. Even if not in the final submission, it is a helpful part of the organizing of a portfolio for the candidate to establish and record his or her continuing learning needs.

5(a) Identifying and taking up learning opportunities: growth

This section may also be part of the working process of the portfolio rather than being presented for submission to an assessor. It forms part of the candidate's plan and so it is important that it is done. The candidate, with the guidance of the mentor, should decide whether to include this information.

5(b) Identifying and taking up learning opportunities: review

A summary to review the outcomes of the work undertaken by the candidate is an important part of the portfolio, especially where the outcomes provide supportive evidence. Dates should be given for all the sections. The review may be seen as a follow-up to what has been presented, so the date will give an idea of the development process.

An example of a professional development portfolio

Drawing on a previous example, here is an illustration of what part of a portfolio might consist of if submitted by a candidate for accreditation with the MCI.

One alternative to the way this portfolio was organized is to keep all the descriptions of one experience together with the evidence and action. As long as the portfolio is in a flexible form, and the headings are broadly similar to the ones described, it can be put together in the most helpful order.

This kind of portfolio illustrates not just what somebody did, with evidence to satisfy the assessor, but also shows the development process. We can see that this person has attained new skills by managing her own development. The assessor would also be able to see the practical and positive effect of this person's work on the team and organization.

The required competences listed and cross-referenced with the experience and the evidence will enable the assessor to make a judgement as to how far the candidate has demonstrated her abilities in those areas. It would be helpful for a portfolio to illustrate at least two cases where a particular element of competence can be demonstrated. The assessor will look carefully at the range indicators detailed in the competence statements to see if they match what has been presented, so the portfolio should be organized to assist that search.

PORTFOLIO OF *Caroline Burgener*
ADDRESS *98 Gatsby Road, Plowden*
WORK *Team Leader, Matthew Reeves plc, civil engineering consultants, Hagley.*
PURPOSE OF PORTFOLIO *Personal development and to submit as evidence of competence for MCI: Management Level I*
DATE PORTFOLIO STARTED *22 May 1993*
OTHERS INVOLVED *Martin Spriggs, mentor; Duncan Lipscombe, line manager*
Angie Mattingley, mentor; Linda Gordon, internal assessor
THE ORGANIZATION
Matthew Reeves plc is an international company with offices throughout Europe and North America. Its head office in Lancashire employs 220 people engaged mainly on civil engineering contracts in the UK. Some overseas contracts are developed here.
An organization structure chart is attached, together with an information brochure about the company.
MY ROLE
As a team leader, I am responsible for overseeing projects designated to me, allocating tasks and roles, ensuring that resources are available, working to a timetable and ensuring that the work is undertaken to time, to the customer's specification and within budget.

CONTENTS:

SECTION	TOPIC	PAGE Nos.
A	*INDEX*	*1-2*
B	*EXPERIENCES AND LEARNING*	*3-15*
C	*EVIDENCE*	*25-40*
D	*LEARNING NEEDS AND ACTION*	*50-60*
E	*ACTION TAKEN AND REVIEW*	*70-80*

SECTION A   PAGE 1
INDEX

Note: MCI references are to Level, Unit and Element.
Thus: I 4.2 refers to Management Level I, Unit 4, Element 2 which states "contribute to the assessment and selection of candidates against team and organisational requirements".

SECTION B   PAGE 10   DATE *3 June 1993*

EXPERIENCE   *Being a team leader for the first time*

REFERENCE MCI COMPETENCES:
Unit I 5 Develop teams, individuals and self to enhance performance
  Element I 5.1 Develop and improve teams through planning and activities
  Element I 5..3 Develop oneself within the job role

Unit I 7 Create, maintain & enhance effective working relationships
  Element I 7.1 Establish & maintain the trust & support of one's subordinates
  Element I 7..2 Establish & maintain the trust & support of immediate manager

Unit I 9 Exchange information to solve problems & make decisions
  Element I 9.1 Lead meetings & group discussions to solve problems & make decisions

DESCRIPTION OF EXPERIENCE
When I was promoted to being team leader for the first time, I was petrified that I'd get things wrong. I was worried that I couldn't ask any of the team for advice because I thought that they would ridicule me and not give me any respect in the future. I hadn't realized at the time that they would have provided me with a lot of support. It probably took about six months longer than it needed to get things really going with our project because it took so long for me to trust the team (and myself) well enough to share ideas around.

WHAT I LEARNT FROM THIS
I learnt to trust people more and to expect the best of them. I also learnt to consult more with colleagues and to ask questions and share ideas. I think I've also learnt to have more confidence in myself.

SECTION C   PAGE 32   DATE *2 August 1993*

EVIDENCE   *Being a team leader for the first time*

○ *Two months ago I was asked to lead a project team to draw up plans for a new proposal we have been asked to tender for. I got the team together and we started by having a brain-storming session. This stimulated a lot of ideas and enthusiasm, mainly because it was a different way of working for most of them. The end result was that we came up with a good plan and a lot of commitment from the team to go forward with the proposal. I'd never have worked with the team this way before. I didn't have the confidence.*

I enclose in my portfolio:
1. *the plans we drew up*
2. *the notes from the brain-storming session that show all the ideas*
3. *the timetable for the latest project, compared with the previous programme that took far longer to complete.*
4. *questionnaires from team members saying how they assess my leadership*
5. *a letter from my manager complimenting me*
6. *a copy of the tender and the contract showing it was accepted*
7. *my checklist of aims for meetings*
8. *meeting agenda drawn up by me*
○ 9. *minutes of meeting I chaired showing decisions reached and action points*
10. *self evaluation "before & after" chart*
11. *timetable for self development, with comments from training manager*

SECTION D   PAGE 55   DATE *3 August 1993*

LEARNING NEEDS   *Being a team leader for the first time*

○ *Having begun to work with teams in this way, I saw that I could do more. I needed to gain some skills in working with a group; to get some more discipline in our discussion and arriving at decisions. Two things in particular: one in running meetings better, the other in getting the information into a better order so as to arrive at the best conclusions. The second part seemed to be about analysing and planning, but being able to do that on the spot and with the team rather than after the meeting on my own.*

ACTION PLAN

I talked to our training manager to see what courses were available on meetings skills or if I could get hold of one of the videos that we have access to or at least find something to read. Apart from that, I needed to get some more practical experience. I discussed with my own manager ways in which I could chair some of the other meetings that he currently
○ *runs, or at least co-chair some with him. I would concentrate on the things I needed to improve, getting more order into the decision making and being able to analyse the information. I drew up a "before and after" chart so as to judge how I did. I agreed with my line manager and our training manager a timetable so that I could do what I wanted to do in three months.*

SECTION E   PAGE 77   DATE *20 November 1993*

ACTION TAKEN   *Being a team leader for the first time*
It took a bit longer than I thought. I finally managed to get on to a training course on meetings which was really
helpful and gave me a lot of practice and ideas about where I can improve things. Mostly, it confirmed that what I've
been doing over the past three months has been quite good. I did a checklist for myself of what I want to be achieving at
my meetings. I have put that into my portfolio. This helped me to get a proper agenda and keep to the topics better. Several
people have commented on how the meetings have improved and it showed at our last one when we got through some very
tricky decisions that we needed to make. My manager was very supportive and encouraged me to get involved in other
meetings and even asked me to chair a new quality team meeting where most people were senior to me. It was quite nerve-
racking but it went very well and I got several congratulations.

REVIEW   DATE *10 January 1994*
I believe that the evidence enclosed with this portfolio, and listed on page 32, gives ample proof of my competence in the
MCI Level I Units and Elements shown on page 10. Further corroboration may be obtained from the individuals
described on the front of this portfolio and our training manager.
Since undertaking the work described as "being a team leader for the first time", additional outcomes have been that our
team, with me at the head, has been allocated a major new project, and that this was gained by the company on the
strength and quality of our previous work. I was also asked by my manager to coach new team leaders in developing
their teams. Evidence of this is added to section C.

Team development

Portfolios intended for team development are rather different.
They are not intended to replace individual portfolios, but rather
to enhance them. They will be held by individuals in the team and
there will be items that are specific to particular members of the
team. The material that goes into portfolios for team development
will relate to experiences and issues dealt with in the team, and
learning and action that has taken place in the team setting.

The organizing of a team portfolio depends on the needs of the
team and the objectives it sets for its own development. Use the
portfolio model for team development, described in Chapter 4, to
help in deciding how to put a portfolio together.

Members of a team may be a group who work together or who
have similar functional responsibilities but are perhaps working in
different parts of the same organization. The former will have regular contact, the latter may well only come together for team meetings. Whatever the purpose and membership of the team, there is
a quite distinct process for portfolio development that means that
there must be a time set aside, either at a separate meeting or
within a regular team meeting, for this work.

What will help is the inclusion of a 'portfolio review' meeting or
item on each agenda; and the provision of a portfolio folder or

binder for each member of the team. The portfolio itself should include briefing notes and prepared forms to aid consistency in presentation. The 'jotter pad' (Figure 5.1) is an example of something that might be helpful.

The front of the portfolio should give information about the organization, the team and the individual owner's name and details. Although the portfolio process in this case is primarily intended for team development, each portfolio is the property of the individual. Some organizations may wish, for reasons of confidentiality, to put limitations on ownership, but this should be the exception rather than the rule.

The portfolio cover information should also include the composition of the team, including the team leader or facilitator, the purpose for the portfolio, the contract agreed and any specific targets set, together with dates. A team portfolio may be developed for one particular project or purpose over a limited period. The individual will be able to take his or her portfolio on to another team or project within the same (or even a different) organization so that the development process continues and is spread. The organizing of the portfolio should allow for that flexibility and continuation of use.

The portfolio structure can mirror the team development process.

1. Strengths: 'what we have'

This is a 'starting from strengths' approach, so begin the content of the portfolio with the strengths of the team. They can be listed to show the combined strengths, with a system to indicate who has which particular abilities and interests. It should be added to regularly as people gain new competences or new people join the team. This is an ideal way of new people becoming familiar with the team and vice versa.

2. The competences required of us: 'what we need'

This section is based on the objectives and targets set for or by the team. It provides the opportunity for everyone to see and to take responsibility for the additional competences needed.

The information in the portfolio indicates what is required overall: who is to take what action, by when, to gain the required competences. It also highlights any area that the portfolio's owner needs to develop personally.

3. Action and training: 'what we did and what we learnt'

Individuals who were responsible for taking any action, which might include training in particular skills, will report back on the outcomes to the rest of the team. There may be lessons to be learnt by others, and there may be implications for further action by other members of the team.

The results of the action and learning should be documented by each member, with indications showing if and how that particular person was involved in the direct learning process.

4. Team review: 'how we've done'

At an agreed regular interval, the team will assess its overall performance against the work targets specified within the portfolio. This section will record the assessment, showing tangible evidence to support it – for example, copies of productivity results, comparative figures, project outcomes etc.

There may be new targets as a result of the review. Those should be included in this section of the portfolio and transferred to the appropriate section at the front.

5. Appraisal: 'what have we gained and what's next?'

Two of the greatest motivators and sources of personal satisfaction are known to be the personal recognition gained from having achieved a challenge and a positive appraisal from one's boss or team colleagues. This indicates the importance of ensuring that opportunities are provided for that and that a record is kept of the feedback made and given.

The appraisal in portfolio development is a team process. Individuals give and receive feedback and the team as a whole assesses its own development and where it needs to improve its performance. This section should contain the appraisal comments made to the individual portfolio holder, together with a personal assessment and what he or she needs to do next. It will also include a summary of the progress made by the team and the agreed next development stage. See Chapter 12 for ideas on organizing a team portfolio.

Organization development

An organization's portfolio would normally refer to its products and services and be used as a part of its marketing strategy. Most organizations have some kind of portfolio; at the very least a leaflet or brochure outlining what is offered to customers. A portfolio for organization development looks rather different and has a different purpose, although the intended outcome is towards the enhancement of products and services.

The process described in Chapter 5 and illustrated in Figure 5.2 is the basis for organizing the portfolio. The preliminary question is, who is to make the decisions about what goes into the portfolio for development? In the healthiest of organizations, this will be a cross-section of staff, customers and others involved. Where the culture for this does not exist, it is more likely that a senior management team will draw together the development portfolio.

The front of the portfolio should describe the organization, the people involved in putting it together and the process of information collection that went into its compilation. It should also have the date of its production. A new development portfolio should be produced on a yearly cycle on average.

The portfolio should be made available, at least in summary form, to everyone in the organization. It is the organization's key statement of its commitment to its own and its members' development.

1. Values and aims: 'why are we doing this?'

The first section within the portfolio needs to describe succinctly and clearly the organization's values and aims for the next period of, say, three to five years. It should go on to describe how it plans to adhere to those values and achieve its aims. Shorter term objectives should indicate how the aims are to be met.

This is a normal part of what an organization should do anyway. If it does, it is easy to put its statements into a portfolio. If it doesn't, the portfolio will become a good discipline.

2. Human resources: 'who have we got?'

This section should concentrate on the people available. In large organizations this will be a summary of the main functions and strengths of the staff in the different departments or locations. The portfolio needs to be in a flexible form so that the individual departments and the teams within those departments can relate this to their own strengths in more detail.

There are two main purposes for this summary of human resources: the first is to trigger off the process of team portfolio development and act as a catalyst for teams to discover their strengths; the second is for the organization to keep track of its personnel development plan.

3. Needs analysis: 'what have they got and what do they need?'

This is an essential activity within any organization. With the advent and development of quality and competence requirements, organizations will either have a set of guidelines to which they subscribe or they will need to develop their own. The portfolio will show what competences already exist. It will also show which ones are needed in order to achieve the required standards and quality designated by the relevant external body and the organization.

The size of the organization will determine the content of the portfolio and how it is structured. The details in a large organization will be contained within the individual and team portfolios, with information being fed in, analysed and summarized. While the organization can define its overall requirements and transmit those to the staff at different levels, it also needs to obtain information of what is required and available in its different parts. This means that the portfolio must be arranged to give and receive information. It becomes not only a flexible document but also a dynamic one, moving between groups and levels within the organization and changing as it does so.

4. Development plan: 'how can we provide the learning structure?'

The development plan is the statement of intent and a description of how the organization is to encourage all its staff to achieve constant growth and improvement. It will indicate the learning process and the structures, systems and resources that will be put into place over the following year or so.

In making provision for a portfolio approach, the plan will need to show how the links will be made between the individual, the team and the organization, and describe the responsibilities of each in making the plan work.

5. Organization review: 'how have we done; what can we change?'

The review process for the organization is a continual one. A constant stream of information flows up and down, backwards and forwards. This section is a 'snapshot' of its progress at a particular point, usually on an annual basis.

There will be many examples of excellent and improving practices, and no doubt some examples of where things went wrong. All can be learnt from. The portfolio itself draws from those examples and selects some that will provide a good illustration of how individual and team initiatives have had an impact on the rest of the organization.

Where decisions have been made to change some practices, these are shown in this section. In some cases this may lead to a change of aims or shorter term objectives and often of strategy. The portfolio should acknowledge such changes, including the practical ones – for example, a change in a production method or office design, and the deeper changes that may take place. Such changes can affect the culture. This should be recorded in the portfolio to demonstrate the real success and progress of the organization.

Chapter 11

A Culture Change – Making it Real

In my introduction, I gave as one of the implications of developing a portfolio approach the possibility of a changed organizational culture. Culture change within organizations has been presented almost as a hopeful myth; we say we want it, but few people claim to have seen it happen and most don't believe it's real.

In this chapter I will look at:

1. what a culture change means;
2. the impact of the portfolio approach on an organization's culture;
3. how portfolios help in working within an environment of change; and
4. the culture within which a portfolio approach will thrive.

What does a culture change mean?

First, you may want to look at your own organization and ask a few questions. Here is a questionnaire designed for the purpose. Rate each question on how satisfied you are.

Scores are: 5 if you are extremely satisfied
                    4 if you have a high level of satisfaction
                    3 if you are reasonably satisfied
                    2 if you are dissatisfied
                    1 if you are very dissatisfied with the situation.

ORGANIZATION CULTURE QUESTIONNAIRE

SECTION ONE: COMMUNICATION

1. How good are people at talking to one another in the organization?   ....
2. How good are people at listening to each other?   ....
3. How good are people at passing on information?   ....
4. How much openness exists?   ....
5. How well do people give and receive direct feedback?   ....
6. How well do meetings work?   ....
7. How good is the communication across and between hierarchies?   ....
8. How good is communication between customers and the organization?   ....
9. How well do people share ideas?   ....
10. How is conflict dealt with?   ....

SECTION TWO: FINANCE

11. How are salary/wage differentials worked out?   ....
12. How close to functions are levels of budgetary responsibility?   ....
13. Is there good accountability for spending and earning?   ....
14. Is financial information shared?   ....
15. Are there profit-sharing schemes?   ....
16. Are there other positive financial incentives?   ....

SECTION THREE: DECISION TAKING

17. Are decisions taken at appropriate levels?   ....
18. Is there a good consultation process?   ....
19. How well are decisions communicated?   ....
20. Are decisions implemented effectively?   ....

SECTION FOUR: STAFF DEVELOPMENT

21. Is there a positive equal opportunities policy and practice?   ....
22. Is there a career development process for staff?   ....
23. Is there a good recruitment and selection process?   ....
24. What is the induction process like?   ....
25. Do people learn in the organization?   ....
26. Are there good opportunities for training?   ....
27. Is coaching a normal part of managers' duties?   ....

28. Is there a positive appraisal system in operation?   ....
29. Is there a satisfactory grievance procedure for staff?   ....
30. How are disciplinary matters dealt with?   ....
31. Is there a staff welfare programme?   ....
32. Is there a counselling programme?   ....
33. Is redundancy dealt with satisfactorily?   ....

SECTION FIVE: THE WORK ENVIRONMENT

34. Are the work surroundings and conditions safe, pleasant and healthy?   ....
35. Is there adequate consultation about the work environment?   ....
36. Is action carried out promptly to improve conditions when needed?   ....
37. Do people take on responsibility for their own work environment?   ....
38. Are there good facilities for people for rest and recreation?   ....

SECTION SIX: COMMUNITY

39. Is there good contact with the surrounding community?   ....
40. Is there an involvement with the local community?   ....

TOTAL SCORES   ....

What is your satisfaction rating of the organization's culture? The total scores give you a rough guide to how you think it is doing.

If you gave 40–80 why are you still there? Not much is likely to change.

A score of 81–100 shows that some radical rethinking is needed, but there may be a chance.

101–120 indicates plenty of room for improvement; the portfolio approach can work with care.

121–160 shows an organization with a very positive culture ready for the portfolio approach now.

If you have 161–200 you work in the perfect organization; or you're kidding!

Whatever your score, you will have a notion as to the kind of culture that exists and the sort of changes that you would like to make. The questionnaire may have helped to define some specific areas, but making a culture change means much more than dealing with the details. It means a whole way of working.

In the management magazine *Human Resources* (Summer 1993), Godfrey Golzen interviewed Ricardo Semler, a young Brazilian industrialist. Semler totally refashioned his father's engineering company, Semco, when he took it over and transformed it from a struggling to a highly successful and profitable business. Semler has described his approach, called business process re-engineering, in his book *Maverick!* Hierarchies are broken down radically, there is wide consultation on important decisions, upward appraisal is common. People even set their own salary levels and expenses, as long as they can justify them. There is no formal training programme. Instead, 'people are encouraged to think about the skills they will need and training for those is available on demand, but Semco will only pay for it if it is going to benefit the company.'

Culture changes go on constantly, although often we may not notice them. There are four broad areas that have changed radically over the past ten to fifteen years that have affected society through its organizations as well as its individuals.

1. Changes in the kind of work

In the UK and other industrialized nations there has been a manufacturing decline, accompanied by the growth in technology and an expansion in service industries. This has had an enormous impact on the kinds of competences people need to be successful in work.

2. Changes in work patterns

The eighties and the nineties have seen a shift away from large organizations employing people in jobs for life towards a contract culture, where organizations and individuals compete with each other to gain work. Self-employment, small businesses, part-time work and unemployment are much more part of a cultural norm than before.

3. Equal opportunities

Assisted by legislation, there is a much greater awareness of the importance of providing equality of opportunity for people who may otherwise face a disadvantage. Practice is somewhat further behind, but pragmatism as well as social conscience has seen significant changes, including some increase in the numbers of women in jobs previously seen as male preserves.

4. The environment

Few people would now treat resources as though they were inexhaustible. Much more is talked about than acted upon; nevertheless there has been a great change in awareness and in some practice, particularly in the production of consumables.

All of those changes have meant that attitudes and behaviour have changed in ways that have hardly been noticeable. Yet the changes have been radical and far reaching. Few organizations operating successfully today will have got there by acting in the same way that they did ten or even five or fewer years ago.

The impact of the portfolio approach on an organization's culture

Empowerment

The portfolio approach is an empowering approach. Used in the way I have described, it will have an impact on the organization's culture. Above all, people are likely to feel empowered to take greater responsibility for their work and to contribute more to the overall well-being of the organization as well as themselves.

Using portfolios for individual, team and organization development will have an impact on each of the sections of the questionnaire that you have just looked at. Here are some of the possible implications of an integrated portfolio approach. It will be as well for you and the other key people in your organization to be pre-pared for them.

Communication

Even a limited exercise to test out a portfolio approach will lead to people communicating more about the things that have a bearing on them within their work. Not all of the communication will be comfortable. People may well hear things that they don't like or want to avoid. Sharing portfolios, particularly within teams, will show how people can communicate productively and positively even where there are negative things to say.

Finance

Some potential culture changes are radical; for some organizations too radical to contemplate. People at all levels becoming account-able for their own budgets, even their own salaries and expense accounts, sounds a trifle dangerous. Yet where people are encour-aged to share their ideas, develop their abilities, take action on real work issues and see that their ideas have an impact on the organi-zation, anything is possible. Management theorists like Rosabeth Moss-Kanter, Tom Peters and others have been saying this for a long time. Business practitioners like Ricardo Semler show that it works in practice.

Decisions

The same goes for the decision-making process. People taking decisions at the level that counts, rather than having to go through bureaucratic ranks of gatekeepers, enables things to happen. The adoption of a portfolio approach makes people throughout the organization aware of the action needed to improve things. Since the portfolio is a constant monitoring system, it means that the results of decisions and action will quickly be seen, encouraging more ideas and more action.

Staff development

The clearest changes are likely to be in this area. One of the ironies of the training revolution is that, in a portfolio approach, there may be less training and more learning. Rather than a blanket training programme being offered to staff, people will develop their portfolios and themselves by learning in many different ways. The very process of portfolio development is a learning one. Training will be focused on what people actually need in relation to the competences required of them in their work. While the resources need to be there for staff development, it will be a self-managed development, rather than a series of training course attendances.

The work environment

The outcome of people becoming more responsible for their own management, their own development and their own outputs is that they also become more responsible for their own work environment. No longer will staff bemoan the fact that nobody has allowed them that change of office furniture; they will be and feel responsible for doing something about it if they can justify it within their own budgets.

Community

Finally, one of the results of a more integrated and healthy organization is that it tends to look outwards. Organizations who contribute to the community around them, beyond the course of their normal business, find that the benefits are satisfyingly mutual.

These culture changes can take place without the introduction of a portfolio approach. Equally, not all of those changes are the automatic result of portfolio development. I suggest that a portfolio approach will almost certainly cause significant changes, because it changes the dynamic of the relationship between teams, between managers and staff, and between the individual and the organization.

How portfolios help in working within an environment of change

Many organizations are going through big changes during this decade. Public service organizations in Britain, once managed by the State, have become or are going though the process of being privatized. Large organizations are being broken down or, conversely, smaller organizations are being merged with each other. Once apparently invulnerable businesses are finding the going tough, or have closed down altogether. Almost everywhere management levels and bureaucratic systems are being streamlined. In this climate of change, how can the introduction of yet another apparent change be of help?

One way in which a portfolio approach can help is for it to be introduced as part of the whole developmental process rather than as a separate method to do with training. Whether portfolios are about personal, professional, team or organization development, or all four, the approach can assist any change process.

Personal

Individuals working within an environment of change inevitably go through uncertainty and apprehension, with all the negativity that these feelings can cause. They may be in fear of losing their jobs, they may have anxiety about what they can offer in a changed situation. Having the opportunity to develop a personal portfolio is a means of gaining a more positive self-image. It helps people to know what they have to offer, which will be useful in the event of their finding themselves in a different situation inside or outside the organization. It will also give them a greater ability to take control of their future.

Professional

Portfolio-building for professional development will help people to give a practical demonstration of their competences and to gain nationally recognized qualifications. In times of change it becomes increasingly important for people to know that they have something tangible that will be sought after. The confidence that this engenders can have a significant bearing on how they sell themselves and their skills and ideas to their employers, their customers and their colleagues.

Team

The hopes and fears of impending or current change are nowhere more apparent than within the team. This is where rumours, conflict, disenchantment and pessimism are at their most obvious. The development of a portfolio approach will allow those issues to be faced in an open and healthy way. The joint recognition of strengths, coupled with the ability to take action on the work issues that directly affect them, will enable the team to see change as a challenge rather than a threat.

Organization

The organization that takes on a portfolio approach for itself will be in a far better position to deal with change than one that sees portfolios simply as an individual staff development method. The changes likely to come about through the implementation of an integrated portfolio approach will affect other changes in one of two broad ways. They will either act in a complementary way or as an antidote to the other developments taking place. Where the changes include opening up the management structure, improving communication and raising quality standards, the portfolio approach will be a natural accompaniment. On the other hand, where the changes are to do with rationalization of the kind that moves people out or around without any consultation or consideration of the impact upon them, a portfolio approach would confront managers with the need to think more deeply about the potential damage. Of course, in the latter scenario, a portfolio approach is hardly likely to be on the agenda.

The culture within which a portfolio approach will thrive

There is a bit of 'chicken or egg' about this. Do you start with a positive organizational culture before developing a portfolio approach, or do you set up a portfolio approach in the hope of developing a positive culture? The answer is, of course, it all depends. What should be clear is that a portfolio approach will not exist without a healthy organization culture and that a portfolio approach will make a big contribution to that culture.

The vital factor is a commitment by the key policy makers and all those whose task it will be to implement and support portfolio development and its consequences. I have tried to show that portfolios for development go far beyond the idea of getting staff up to certain quality standards. If you accept and become committed to the notion that portfolio development is a route to development for all, corporately as well as individually, your action will reflect that commitment.

Chapter 12

Exercises

This chapter describes some of the exercises and activities that you could develop for individual, team and organization portfolios. While some are designed to be used by individuals or teams on their own, they will all need the support of someone (mentor, adviser, facilitator etc) who will be able to take people through the process for at least the first few times. All the material is based on that used over the past seven years during the course of my involvement with portfolio development in a range of settings. You can adapt the questions to suit your own requirements. Remember to allow space for people to make their own recordings.

Individual portfolio development

The material included here is useful for personal or professional development. The main difference is in step 4, where the competences defined will be drawn, in the case of professional development, from the accreditation body's competence requirements.

AN INDEX OF EXPERIENCES

Activity   Compile a list of personal experiences, each described in one or two words, as a brief reminder. The experiences should be those which seem to you to have been significant and which in some way contributed to your current understanding, skills and knowledge. The list should be as wide as possible; to help with this, the list should be completed under five broad headings:

EDUCATION TRAINING (include formal and informal)	WORK (include full time, part time, voluntary)	PROJECTS (include anything that you have undertaken)	LEISURE (include travel, sports, reading etc)	LIFE EVENTS (include anything of significance to you)

This list now becomes the Index of your Personal Portfolio. Each item should be numbered.
Note: You will add to this index as you recall or gain other experiences.

A PORTFOLIO OF PRIOR LEARNING EXPERIENCES

Step 1: DESCRIBING EXPERIENCE

Activity: Select one specific experience from your own index. This can be an experience from any broad heading and can be a 'positive' or a 'negative' experience.

Having made the selection, describe the experience to someone else. This person may be your manager, supervisor, tutor or a colleague, acting as a mentor. The important thing is that the role of this person is to listen to you describing the experience and help you to summarize and record it here.

(space for recordings here)

Name: **Date:**

RECORDED EXPERIENCE (No. on Index).......

Time suggested: 15–20 minutes. **The summary should go into your Portfolio.**

Step 2: LEARNING FROM EXPERIENCE

Activity: Consider the learning you have gained from the specific experience just described. This should again be with the listening support of someone else, who should ask what you have learnt from the experience and how the learning was gained. As before, you should summarize and record the learning.

Name: **Date:**

RECORDED EXPERIENCE (No. on Index).......

LEARNING GAINED

(space for recordings here)

Time suggested: 15–20 minutes. **The summary should go into your Portfolio.**

Step 3: DEMONSTRATING COMPETENCES

Activity: Put together evidence to show how you now use the learning that has just been recorded. The evidence should properly demonstrate how learning is used. Evidence can be direct, through examples of your work or through written, photographic or other recorded evidence; or indirect, with other people providing information and references.

SUMMARY OF EVIDENCE TO DEMONSTRATE HOW LEARN-ING IS NOW USED

(space for recordings here)

Step 4:   LEARNING NEEDS
THE REQUIREMENTS OF MY CURRENT AND POSSIBLE
FUTURE WORK FOR WHICH I HAVE NOT YET DEMON-
STRATED MY COMPETENCE ARE: (LIST)
1.
2.
3. etc

MY FURTHER LEARNING NEEDS ARE:
1.
2.
3. etc

Step 5:   DEVELOPING A LEARNING PROGRAMME
Activity: Consider which of the continuing learning needs are
priorities in terms of
(a) importance to current work
(b) importance for future work
(c) interest
With the help of your supervisor or trainer, you should then
investigate and decide upon which kind of learning opportunity to
take up. This might range from reading an article or practising a
specified skill under tuition, to taking up a degree course. The
appropriate learning opportunity should then be negotiated with your
employer and taken up.
Name: **Date:**
MY PRIORITIES FOR LEARNING ARE: (IN RANK ORDER)
1.
2.
3. etc

THE FOLLOWING LEARNING HAS BEEN COMPLETED AND
CAN BE INCLUDED AS PART OF MY EXPERIENCE:
(*space for recordings here*)

Team portfolio development

The following material is drawn from work with one particular
organization. You may want to adapt the the terms used to reflect
the ones used by your organization and the purpose for which the

portfolio is to be used. In this case, the emphasis was on heightening awareness to the customer at every level within the organization.

A PORTFOLIO

OUR AIM is to improve the quality of our service to the customer and therefore of our overall business performance continually. In order to do this we want to improve how we learn from the customer. Each one of us from office cleaner to managing director is a vital link in the chain; each one of us provides a service to customers; we are also each other's customer.

THE PURPOSE of this portfolio is for us to learn from each other, and therefore to learn from the customer how we can improve. The portfolio is yours; for you to keep a record of what you see, what you do and what you learn from your contact with your customers and colleagues at work. It's also to be shared with the other members of your working group, so that they learn along with you how to improve things.

THERE ARE THREE STAGES in building up your portfolio:
1. For you to record a summary of your learning experiences from customer contact in the pages of your portfolio as indicated. At first you will find it useful to discuss these experiences with a helper (see guidelines).
2. For you to meet with your working group on a regular basis, discuss with them what has gone into your portfolio (or someone else's portfolio) and what action needs to be taken to improve things.
3. For you to note in your portfolio at a later date what has improved and how you can demonstrate this by adding evidence to your portfolio.

NAME...DATE........................
LOCATION..
MY NOTES OF WHAT I DID OR SAW

> ### WHO IS THE CUSTOMER?

> ### WHAT HAPPENED?

> ### WHY DID IT HAPPEN?

> ### WHO WILL I DISCUSS THIS WITH AND WHEN?

SHARING THE LEARNING

> ### WHAT HAVE I LEARNED FROM THIS?

> ### HOW WILL I DEAL WITH THIS IN THE FUTURE?

> ### WHAT CAN OTHERS LEARN FROM THIS?

WHEN I WILL DISCUSS THIS WITH MY GROUP

GROUP DISCUSSION

DATE.............................

GROUP COMMENTS

HOW HAS THE GROUP'S REACTION CHANGED

MY UNDERSTANDING?

WHAT ACTION HAS BEEN AGREED?

RESULTS

DATE................................

WHAT HAS HAPPENED TO IMPROVE THINGS?

HOW CAN I DEMONSTRATE THESE IMPROVEMENTS?

(GIVE EXAMPLES)

Organization portfolio development

These exercises are intended for the key decision makers; the ones who will be supporting and making the resources available for the portfolio approach to development and who will be instrumental in ensuring that it works through their own commitment to it. The questions can be asked of people individually or through a questionnaire, or can form the basis of a workshop session with the senior management team.

Values and aims

- How do we now agree our values and aims?
- What are our values and aims?
- Do we have them written down in an acceptable format? If so, where are they?
- How do we present our values and aims to staff and customers?

Human resources

- How do we now establish our own current strengths and those of staff?
- What are our own current strengths?
- What are the main strengths of our staff?

Needs analysis

- What are the strengths we will need in the future?
- What strengths will staff need in the future?

Development plan

- How do we now go about planning our staff development needs?
- What is our staff development plan, and what are the processes that we use?

Organization review

- How do we review our progress?
- How do we learn as an organization?
- What improvements do we want to make in the way the organization develops?

References

Armstrong, Michael (1993) *Managing Human Resources*, Kogan Page.

Bolger, Steve and Scott, Duncan (1984) *Starting From Strengths*, National Youth Bureau.

Boydell, Tom, Burgoyne, John and Pedlar, Mike (1991) *The Learning Company*, McGraw-Hill.

Collard, Ron (1993) *Total Quality: Success Through People*, Institute of Personnel Management.

Cowling, Alan and Mailer, Chloe (eds) (1992) *Managing Human Resources*, Edward Arnold.

Critten, Peter (1993) *Investing in People: Towards Corporate Capability*, Butterworth-Heinemann.

Critten, Peter and Redman, Warren (1990) *Learning from Experience: Building a Learning Organisation*, Employment Department Learning Technologies Unit.

Drucker, Peter (1978) *People and Performance*, Heinemann.

Drucker, Peter (1993) *Managing for the Future*, Butterworth-Heinemann.

Drummond, Helga (1992) *The Quality Movement*, Kogan Page.

Evans, Norman (1982) *Post Education Society*, Croom Helm.

Fletcher, Shirley (1991) *NVQs, Standards and Competence*, Kogan Page.

Fletcher, Shirley (1993) *Quality and Competence*, Kogan Page.

Garratt, Bob (1987) *The Learning Organisation*, Gower.

Handy, Charles (1990) *The Age of Unreason*, Arrow.

Handy, Charles (1993) *Understanding Organisations*, Penguin.

Heimler, Eugene (1985) *The Healing Echo*, Souvenir Press.

Henry, Jane (ed) (1991) *Creative Management*, Sage Publications.

Keeton, Maurice and Tate, Pamela (1978) *Learning by Experience*, Jossey-Bass.

Kolb, David (1976) *Learning Styles Inventory*, McBer and Co.

Mabey, Christopher and Mayon-White, Bill (eds) (1993) *Managing Change*, Open University Press.

Marshall, Janice (1993) *Portfolio Development*, Development Processes Ltd.

Moss-Kanter, Rosabeth (1988) *The Change Masters*, Unwin Hyman.

Peters, Tom (1992) *Liberation Management*, Macmillan.

Redman, Warren (1986) *Knowing What You Know*, National Council of YMCAs.

Redman, Warren and Rogers, Alan (1988) *Show What You Know*, National Youth Bureau.

Robson, Mike (1988) *Quality Circles*, Gower.

Robson, Mike (1993) *Problem Solving in Groups*, Gower.

Savage, Peter (1987) *Who Cares Wins*, Mercury.

Semler, Ricardo (1993) *Maverick!*, Century.

Simosko, Susan (1991) *APL: A Practical Guide for Professionals*, Kogan Page.

Wille, Edgar (1992) *Quality: Achieving Excellence*, Century Business.

Willingham, Warren (1975) *Principles of Good Practice in Assessing Experiential Learning*, CAEL.

Index